Social Awareness in Counselling

✦

A Critique of Mainstream Counselling From A Feminist Counselling, Cross-Cultural Counselling, And Liberation Psychology Perspective

Lucy Costigan

iUniverse, Inc.
New York Lincoln Shanghai

Social Awareness in Counselling

A Critique of Mainstream Counselling From A Feminist Counselling, Cross-Cultural Counselling, And Liberation Psychology Perspective

iUniverse, Inc.

For information address:
iUniverse, Inc.
2021 Pine Lake Road, Suite 100
Lincoln, NE 68512
www.iuniverse.com

ISBN: 0-595-30696-9

Printed in the United States of America

For Bob (Marburg)
With love and a great big thank you
for all your support and guidance
in reviewing and discussing this work.

Contents

Acknowledgements

Thanks to Mary McEvoy of University College Dublin (UCD), Ireland, for your constructive advice, insightful observations and continuous support during the various stages of research, writing and editing for the Masters thesis in Equality Studies which formed the basis of this book.

Also thanks to Kathleen Lynch and all the staff of the UCD Equality Studies faculty for your guidance and support

A big 'thank you' to Michael Cullen for the cover photo of the author, and for all your help with the technical aspects of the book.

Thanks to the Costigans: Anthony, Val, Kathleen, Sharon, Lisa and Antoinette; to the Cullens: Theresa, Sean, Paul and Damien; and to Ray McGovern, for your constant friendship and love.

Hugs to my Irish buddies: Isabel MacMahon, Clara Martin, Carmel Larkin, Maura O'Connor, Andrew Rea, Paddy Meyler, Paul Roche, Rita Murphy and Mary Costin for that old reliable friendship that keeps everything ticking over.

Thanks to my new Californian friends for your friendship and inspiration. Thanks Max Anderson for the insightful art sessions and meditation nights. Thanks to Jennifer Will, Diane Peterite, Vance McCarthy, Sylvester Jernigan, Mark Devenport and Alan Factor for the chats, the dinners and the laughter which are all vital fodder for the creative soul.

Thanks to the following libraries for the use of library and computer facilities:

University College Dublin (UCD), Ireland

University of California at Santa Cruz, USA

University of British Columbia, Vancouver, Canada

Mountain View Public Library, Santa Clara, California, USA.

Cover photo: 'The confession', by Frank Dicksee, 1896 (private collection).

Introduction

Throughout the decade I worked as a counsellor, I began to realise that no one theory could help all people work through their problems. In fact, the only pattern that began to emerge as I watched clients come and go was that those who seemed most like myself—who had similar values, interests, background, and a comparable worldview—were those who seemed the most transformed by my eclectic style of counselling. So I began to ask a number of leading questions: Does counselling have most benefit when the counsellor and the client come from similar social and ethnic backgrounds? What of gender and sexual orientation—what happens when the client's values or experiences are very different from those of the counsellor? Can counselling be of benefit to people who are not very articulate, or is it aimed mainly at well-educated middle-class clients? Does counselling have a place for those who are socially disadvantaged, since the cornerstone of counselling is personal agency and there is never any mention of social responsibility? And what of clients who have been abused or mistreated at the hands of a political dictatorship—what has counselling to offer when society is the cause of their repression and suffering?

For many years I listened as friends, clients and strangers recounted tales of various abuses or irregularities they claimed to have experienced during counselling. These ranged from jeering, insensitive comments made by a counsellor when a female client was feeling most vulnerable, to a male client complaining that his counsellor was still *persuading* him to attend for regular counselling although four years had passed, thousands of dollars had been spent, and little change had occurred in his difficult life situation. I had always been a believer in short-term counselling and wondered how many counsellors could justify routinely seeing people for years, apparently waiting until life could no longer throw up anything to distress or negatively affect them. Abuse and power issues in counselling had never been discussed as part of my training, but of course counselling, like medicine, teaching or any other profession where there is deemed to be an 'expert' and a seeker, requires real awareness of the potential for abuse that may occur at the hands of a power-hungry or sadly misguided individual.

I began to peruse counselling research to see what it had to contribute to these and other related questions. This book is the result of my unearthing of current counselling research. It explores the many areas where mainstream counselling focuses exclusively on the individual while failing to explore wider social issues which often greatly influence our values, behaviours and experiences. Counselling puts little emphasis on the social and cultural factors that greatly shape the way people view themselves and the world around them. Issues such as gender, class, sexual orientation, culture and ethnicity are rarely considered. The social and personal oppression that cultural stereotypes can engender remain largely unacknowledged in mainstream counselling. But let's begin by taking an overview of mainstream counselling.

WHAT DOES MAINSTREAM COUNSELLING PROCLAIM?

Mainstream counselling[1] focuses on the individual's experiences, feelings, needs and present difficulties, and looks at ways of bringing about change in the person's behaviour, attitudes and feelings. The person's family of origin and intimate relationships are also explored. Counselling is rooted in discussing and exploring the client's perceptions and life situation.

Over the last decade counselling has become an established practice in western society where ordinary people who are having problems coping with many aspects of life, such as bereavement, abuse, relationship or work difficulties, can lay down their cares and partake of the empathy and listening skills of a trained counsellor. Counselling as a profession has fought long and hard to be accepted as a reputable body by both state and medical profession. The desire to gain recognition and status for counselling is laced with a huge degree of irony as the origins of counselling are rooted in a deep aspiration to disassociate itself from authoritarian antiquated methods of psychiatry, where the 'normal' model of mental health was based on white, middle-class males.

There are several professional counselling associations now established in Ireland and Britain, such as the Irish Association for Counselling and Psychotherapy (IACP) and the British Association for Counselling and Psychotherapy (BACP), where members are required to undergo certain courses of training and supervised counselling. In Ireland counselling as a profession is still quite fragile, as a counsellor is not required to possess a licence to practice. Counsellors however are now employed by state agencies, such as the Health Board, and in this way seem to have received the much-coveted stamp of approval from the medical profession. In the US most states require that counsellors possess a state licence, denoting that they have undergone rigorous professional training and supervision, and are members of professional organisations.

When it comes to mainstream counselling theories and methods, the variation and diversity between orientations is quite bewildering. The first chapter gives a brief review of the major counselling theories. It begins by giving several definitions of counselling, and then looks at the origins of counselling. Three of the most common forms of counselling are then briefly reviewed in terms of their underlying theoretical frameworks: person-centred counselling, gestalt therapy, and reality therapy. General criticisms of mainstream counselling theories and methods by former counsellors and researchers are also outlined.

ALTERNATIVE COUNSELLING ORIENTATIONS

This book is primarily a critique of mainstream counselling from three alternative therapeutic orientations: feminist counselling, cross-cultural counselling and liberation psychology. A chapter describing the theories and techniques of each is included. Below I have given a brief introduction to each counselling orientation.

Feminist Counselling

The feminist counselling model addresses such issues as gender, class and race, and also emphasises the cultural values and stereotypes which counsellors must be aware of in themselves as well as in their clients. During mainstream counselling there is a preoccupation with the self and with feelings. Counselling has been severely criticised by feminists, cross-cultural counsellors and liberation psychologists for focusing solely on the individual and ignoring the social origins of psychological distress caused by oppression, and for operating as a form of social control (Kitzinger and Perkins: 1993; Masson: 1988; Smail: 1987; Mann: 1987; Szasz: 1961). Many women enter therapy for feelings such as depression, alienation or anxiety, which are clearly linked to oppression, but which counsellors claim to derive from traumas in childhood (Moane: 1999, 3). This may lead to a person becoming enmeshed in an analysis of feelings and personal history, but gaining little constructive insight into the cultural climate that has shaped the significant individuals and relationships in her life.

The structure of the counselling relationship is also worthy of examination. Counselling is a value-laden activity, whereby both counsellor and client each have their own personal values. These values are often culturally based, and it is vital that the counsellor states his or her values to the client at the beginning of counselling. In traditional counselling this does not take place, and so value differences between counsellor and client remain unspoken. This may lead to the counsellor exerting a powerful influence over the client's value system. The feminist counselling model addresses such issues as values, power and equality in the therapeutic relationship.

Cross-cultural Counselling

Increasingly, counsellors in the western world are called upon to work with clients of different cultures. Models derived from mainstream counselling largely ignore any mention of cultural diversity or social difference. Mainstream counsellors inherit the ethos and value system of the dominant western culture. Thus they have little awareness or respect for other traditions, and encounter great difficulty in showing empathy or understanding to clients from other cultures. Cross-cultural counselling is the process of counselling individuals who are of a different culture than that of the therapist (Burn, 1992). Various models are outlined that facilitate cross-cultural counselling by taking account of cultural stereotypes and developing a sensitivity and understanding of differences in cultural practices, communication styles, values, and expectations.

Liberation Psychology

The theories of liberation psychology stress the importance of facing the political, social and economic roots of oppression that limit personal freedom and choice. Liberation psychology was established in the early 1970s in response to the sexism and elitism that permeates traditional psychology. Traditional disciplines of psychology and counselling are largely based on the male, heterosexual, Anglo-Saxon view of human development. This leads to an inherent bias, where the experience of oppressed, marginalised groups is largely ignored in the construction of theories on which counselling is based.

Liberation psychology provides an analysis of the psychological damage associated with oppression. It aims to develop practices that will transform negative psychological patterns, and facilitate taking action to bring about social change (Moane: 1999, 1). Those who write about and practice liberation psychology draw on psychology, feminism, liberation theology, emancipatory education, socialism, and writings on colonialism.

THE FUTURE OF COUNSELLING

After laying bare the various problems that practitioners, counsellors and clients have encountered in counselling, the final chapter highlights areas where change is urgently required if counselling is to grow, develop and transform into a truly caring, healing and empowering profession. The main issues addressed in the last chapter include the necessity of developing a new model of counsellor training, an investigation into the motivation to become a counsellor, and a discussion as to the best type of research for discovering clients' actual experiences in counselling.

Origins and General Criticisms of Mainstream Counselling

DEFINITIONS OF COUNSELLING

The British Association for Counselling and Psychotherapy (Newsome: 1980, 8) gives the following definition of counselling: "People become engaged in counselling when a person occupying regularly or temporarily the role of counsellor offers or agrees explicitly to offer time, attention, and respect to another person or persons temporarily in the role of client. The task of counselling is to give the client an opportunity to explore, discover and clarify ways of living more resourcefully and toward greater well-being."

The Irish "Guide to Counselling and Therapy" (1991, 7) describes counselling as follows: "Counselling is a searching human relationship where you and the counsellor are committed to finding creative responses to your present difficulties and needs. Counselling incorporates the giving of time, attention and respect in a confidential relationship. It provides an opportunity to explore, to discover and to clarify ways of living more resourcefully towards greater well-being."

Murgatroyd (1985, 2) believes that counselling and helping are synonymous. He states that "the aim of counselling and helping is to assist someone to take more control of their life." Barrie Hopson (1981, p. 276) sees counselling as "helping people explore problems so that they can decide what to do about them."

Counselling involves the giving of time, attention and respect by the counsellor to the client, usually for a specified fee (O'Farrell: 1988, 11-17). It provides an opportunity for clients to explore the roots of traumatic experiences in their past or present. The client can then be helped to see patterns in behaviours, feelings, and thoughts that may be contributing to difficulties in all aspects of life. It is envisaged that the client will then become conscious of the choices available to help resolve presenting problems.

ORIGINS OF COUNSELLING

Counselling theories and practices developed as part of humanistic psychology in the United States from the late 1950s onwards. Humanistic psychology was established as a response to the denigration of the human spirit, which had hitherto been implied by the mechanical school of behaviourism[2] and the deterministic psychotherapeutic model of psychoanalysis[3]. Neither behaviourism nor psychoanalysis acknowledged the possibility of studying values, intentions and meanings as elements in the conscious existence of human beings (Association of Humanistic Psychology: 2001).

Humanistic psychology, however, advocated the exploration of individuality, meaning, existentialism, self-actualisation and creativity. It introduced a constructive view of human beings as being largely self-determining, with the capacity to make choices, to be responsible for their actions, and to grow in conscious awareness. These humanistic core values—of personal responsibility, of the ability to make choices, and the potential of the human being to grow in awareness towards self-actualisation—became the cornerstone of the many schools of counselling which were established in the United States from the 1960s onwards. This led to a major shift in the field of mental health, away from medical and psychiatric models of wellness and pathology, towards a new holistic view of the unique self-determining individual.

The counselling methods that derived from humanistic psychology concentrated on the quality of the therapeutic relationship which was developed between counsellor and client. Unlike Freud's psychoanalysis where the 'patient' lies on a couch with eyes closed while the analyst sits listening and observing, in counselling both client and counsellor sit facing each other in a much less formal manner. The counsellor's aim is to create a natural and relaxed setting where the client can begin to open up as though chatting with a friendly confidant.

THEORETICAL FRAMEWORKS USED IN COUNSELLING

The most common forms of counselling and psychotherapy[4] practised today are person-centred counselling, gestalt therapy, and reality therapy. These counselling methods are briefly reviewed below with regard to their theoretical frameworks.

Person-Centred Counselling

Psychologist, Carl Rogers, developed person-centred counselling, which holds that intrinsic tendencies toward self-actualisation can be expressed in a therapeutic relationship in which the therapist offers personal congruence, unconditional positive regard, and accurate empathic understanding. According to Rogers (1961) a client may grow in awareness, and move towards his or her "human potential" through the exploration of life history and current problems with the aid of a therapist "who is psychologically mature". Rogers (1961, 11-12) took the view that the client leads the counsellor in this exploration, as "the client knows what hurts, what direction to go, what problems are crucial, what experiences have been buried".

Through the process of therapy the client moves away from perceiving the self as unacceptable, becomes "transparently real" and finally realises that the "locus of evaluation, the centre of responsibility, lies within himself" (Rogers: 1961, 51-57).

Thus the experience of being understood and valued by the counsellor gives the client the freedom to grow and to live more authentically. This, according to Rogers (1961), is in stark contrast to the onset of pathology which derives from attempting to earn others' positive regard rather than following a personal inner compass.

Gestalt Therapy

Gestalt therapy was developed by Fritz Perls, mainly as an alternative to psychoanalysis and behaviourism. In "Gestalt Therapy Verbatim" (1969), Perls states that individuals should be capable of becoming fully aware of and acting upon their needs. He claims that "awareness is the only basis of knowledge and communication" (1969, 48). The task of the therapist is therefore to awaken awareness in clients by confronting the actual situation in the present moment. Clients are encouraged to pay attention to their inner process—to senses, feelings, imagination and perceptions. By attending to moment to moment changes they discover how they are functioning in their environment.

The basic philosophy of gestalt is existentialist: human beings are free to choose to take responsibility for their destiny. According to O'Leary (1992, 17-18), in gestalt therapy clients are helped to realise that they are responsible for what happens to them. Clients are assisted to move from a position of dependence on others to a state of being self-supporting and independent. They are encouraged to see themselves as having an input into their lives, and to realise that they do in fact have a large degree of control. Growth and awareness is considered to occur when a client begins to open to the possibility of living fully in the present moment.

Reality Therapy

Reality Therapy was devised by William Glasser, an American psychiatrist in the mid 1960s. According to Glasser (1965, 5) "everyone who needs psychiatric treatment suffers from one basic inadequacy: he is unable to fulfil his essential needs." Reality therapy aims to help people find better ways of meeting their needs and taking responsibility for their lives whilst respecting the needs of others. It is mainly concerned with the behaviour a person is using in order to get his or her needs met, but which is leading to problems and lack of fulfilment in life.

In Glasser's opinion, those who have problems in life have a common characteristic "they all deny the reality of the world around them. Some break the law, denying the rules of society" (1965, 6). Glasser advocated a therapy that would help clients to recognise that "reality not only exists but they must fulfil their needs within its framework" (1965, 6). Reality therapy advocates that clients must learn to change, to face the real world, and to learn how to successfully function in that world. According to Glasser (1965, 41), this could be accomplished by the therapist becoming deeply involved in the client's world, encouraging, indeed forcing the client to choose more responsible ways of behaving to achieve desired goals.

Unlike Rogers however, Glasser believed that any exploration of the past was undesirable, as no matter how a person may have been affected by past experiences the only important factor was how he or she could fulfil basic needs in the present.

CRITICISMS OF MAINSTREAM COUNSELLING THEORIES AND METHODS

General criticisms of counselling and psychotherapy have come from many sources. These include counsellors and psychotherapists who have become dissatisfied with the theories and practices which they have been using to treat clients, and various groups which have sought to establish new more egalitarian methods in counselling, such as feminists, cross-cultural counsellors, and liberation psychologists. Critiques of mainstream counselling from each of the feminist, cross-cultural counselling and liberation psychology are dealt with in detail in the remaining chapters. Below are listed general criticisms of mainstream counselling by various counsellors, psychologists and researchers.

Research into Affects of Counselling on Clients

Dineen (1998) states that almost every study ever conducted into the affects of counselling on clients has shown that counselling is no more effective than a placebo, or even no treatment at all. However, research also shows that people who have had therapy feel that it has benefited them in some way, and that surveys have shown "consumer satisfaction" to be quite high among the users of psychotherapy (Dineen: 1998).

A number of reviews across numerous studies indicate that counselling and therapy have a positive effect on clients (Bergin: 1971; Emrick:1977; Luborsky, Singer and Luborsky:1975; Smith and Glass: 1977). However, according to Osipow (1980: 200), the research in many respects has assumed a uniform effect with little regard for specificity of variables, such as type of treatment, goals of treatment, counsellor training, duration of counselling, client problem, outcome criteria, measurement of change and other factors. Evidence of research (Trux and Mitchell: 1977) also indicates that counselling characteristics, such as empathy, warmth and genuineness, are linked to positive client benefit across a variety of counsellors, regardless of theoretical orientation. This research (Trux and Mitchell: 1977) also shows that counsellors who are low on these characteristics seem to account for a vast majority of the deteriorated cases.

According to Saunders (1999) those in the field of psychotherapy research have been eager to establish the "scientific credibility" of therapeutic practice and therefore research has been heavily influenced by the theoretical perspectives of the researcher. The result is that the client's view has never really found a place on the agenda. Most of those involved in researching counselling and psychotherapy have developed their understandings from testing theory, often from a scientific psychological perspective, using more quantitative methods. Polkinghorne (1984) states that this natural science framework, which attempts to examine the client's perspective of counselling tends to examine client variables, or the client as a variable, rather than actually paying attention to the client's view.

McLeod (1998) makes the point that very few people have attempted to conduct research that asks clients what they think about the therapy they are receiving. He suggests the reasons for this can be understood as the convergence of forces within the professional culture surrounding psychotherapy research activity. McLeod argues that strong institutional pressures exist that encourage researchers to follow the assumptions and practices of natural science.

Rowan (1992, 160), suggests that those who are involved in research in psychotherapy have become remote from those who practice it. He goes on to state, "it is difficult for the ordinary person to realise just how irrelevant most of the research actually is". This point is supported by Greenberg (1981), who argues that much of the research in psychotherapy offers little to practicing therapists, as evidence of variables that effect therapeutic outcome is "disappointingly meagre."

Rowan (1992) states that the interesting thing about many studies into the affects of counselling is that they produce no clear results. He concludes that the best controlled studies tell us virtually nothing about psychotherapy as ordinarily practiced and suggests that we have to move to a new paradigm of research which does not even attempt to talk about variables, "……but which talks instead about people, and to people and with people".

The Mystique of Counselling

According to Smail (1978) for the ordinary layperson there is a mystique surrounding mainstream counselling and psychotherapy. The uninitiated often bestow reverence on the therapist, just as in the past the priest and doctor held privileged positions in society. Smail (1978) comments that mainstream psychotherapists and counsellors have done little to puncture this public image of 'expert' in the areas of human behaviour and suffering. What many people do not realise however, is that counsellors and psychotherapists are applying various theories to the treatment of their clients, which are largely taken on trust.

According to Smail (1978, 2-3) the nature of psychotherapy has not been determined by scientific insights into the objective realities of human functioning. Rather, its theories have been built on a mixture of assumptions about what constitutes human health and happiness, combined with ideas about how one person can set about understanding, influencing and changing another.

Thorne (cited in Palmer and Varma: 1997, 155-162), criticises counselling as having become too academic and accreditative, drawing those individuals who desire a lucrative career rather than a passionate vocation. Thorne states that counselling is a very vulnerable professional, and so seeks academic and scientific credibility to prove itself as being 'professional' and its members 'expert'.

Contrasting Theories and Techniques

Psychotherapy and counselling comprise of a wide range of philosophies, theories and techniques which are frequently in marked opposition to each other, and are defended and attacked from deeply entrenched and contrasting ideological positions (Smail: 1978, 3). Psychotherapy may be based on the theories of human development as postulated by Freud, or may be inspired by Roger's person-centred counselling which offers empathic listening. Its aim may be the treatment of clinically depressed clients in a mental hospital, or the resolution of a manager's difficulties with staff in the work place.

In offering an overview of the wide range of psychotherapy approaches, several authors have attempted to group them under broad perspectives (Norcross & Prochaska: 1983; Dryden: 1996; Gelso & Hayes: 1998), such as psychoanalytic/ psychodynamic, humanistic/existential and cognitive[5]/behavioural. Counselling and psychotherapy encompass literally hundreds of approaches to analysis, diagnosis and treatment of clients, while the range, content and severity of problems that clients bring to counselling is enormous.

Smail (1978) states that the differences in approach used in psychotherapy and counselling is quite bewildering. Counsellors may discuss clients' problems in the context of either past events, their present situation or their future goals. If a counsellor focuses on the past, clients are required to retrieve memories from childhood until an incident is recalled which appears to have a direct link with the client's current behaviour and difficulty. Rogers' person-centred counselling is such a model. Criticism of this approach includes the hypothesis that all memories are distorted, and that the best one can achieve is an interpretation of past events (Aveline, cited by Dryden: 1987, 23). Aveline also writes that focusing on the past may provide clients with scapegoats, such as parents, to blame for their present difficulties.

Glasser's reality therapy model focuses almost exclusively on making small changes to one's behaviour in the present, so that goals set can be achieved in the future. Clients are actively discouraged from discussing past experiences. Perl's gestalt therapy focuses on what the client is feeling in the present moment. Gestalt clients are discouraged from intellectualising about the past, but are encouraged to discuss how their feelings in the moment are linked to past experiences. Many counsellors are eclectic, and hence may include an investigation of the past, a discussion of the present, and goal setting for the future in their sessions.

The Artificial Nature of the Counselling Relationship

Masson (1988, 229) states that therapy is by its very nature an artificial relationship, as the exchange of money for a service makes counselling a business transaction. Persaud (1996) voices his concerns that the availability of counselling prevents people from developing their own solutions to problems. He states that counselling may interfere with people struggling with painful issues for long enough so that they finally dig deep and discover solutions for themselves.

Masson (1988, 234) refutes the very concept of Rogers' person-centred counselling, arguing that a counsellor could not possibly be trained to be genuine, empathic, non-judgmental and to have positive regard for a client. Masson (1988) cites incidences of sexual abuse and gross misunderstanding of clients by counsellors. He rebuffs Rogers for his failure to quote incidents where counsellors have breached ethical and professional codes of conduct, and have shown anything but empathy to their vulnerable clients.

Counselling as a Cult

Bruce Charlton (1998) argues that a combination of therapeutic ineffectuality, spiritual arrogance, and moral bankruptcy makes counselling a scandal. According to Charlton (1998), the core of counselling demands that the client makes a confession and brings to light memories of secret or shameful events which are supposed to be the root of current problems. Charlton states that this one-sided confessional relationship is a vital component of many 'brainwashing' techniques, creating an emotional reliance upon the confessor. The more secretive and shameful the things confessed, the greater is the desire for that 'absolution' which only the confessor can give.

Charlton (1998) argues that confessional counselling has no specific therapeutic effectiveness, and that when tested under controlled conditions there is no difference in therapeutic outcome between trained and untrained personnel, and no difference according to length of training or between schools of practice. He states that the therapeutic benefits of counselling are the result of a placebo affect and are non-specifically due to supportive conversation. Expertise in counselling cannot be inculcated, and the techniques and theories (whether Freudian, Jungian, Adlerian, or Rogerian) are irrelevant to effectiveness.

Charlton (1998) also criticises counselling's recruitment policy, where counsellors are largely self-selected. This, he argues, leads to a large number of individuals entering the field whose motivations are suspect. Also, counselling attracts practitioners from those who have suffered emotional and psychological problems and are either consciously or implicitly seeking help for their own difficulties through the counselling relationship.

Charlton (1998) sees the various schools of counselling as a collection of quasi-religious cults, which employ confessional brainwashing techniques to win converts. According to Charlton, although counselling techniques do not have specific therapeutic benefits they often induce distinctive personality changes; in particular, dependence on the therapist and a new way of interpreting human affairs. Such outcomes do not constitute an improvement in personal functioning, he suggests, but an initiation into the role of acolyte. As with any cult, the convert claims vast benefits and positive transformation, while the convert's previous friends and family can see only willful blindness and fanaticism.

Everybody hopes for true friendship with somebody who is kind, understanding, wise and a good listener. Charlton argues, however, that it is absurd to imagine that true friendship can be bought—paid for on an hourly basis, or that its benefits can be encapsulated in a trained technique deployed impartially. Life is frequently difficult and painful, and Charlton refutes that problems of loss, love, sadness and death are amenable to solution by applying a technique of managing conversations.

Charlton (1998) states that counselling is a cult and a confidence trick, which preys upon a wishful craving that the meaning of life can be answered and deep human miseries can be dissolved by 'talking through' problems with a hired expert. His deepest fear is that counselling will become entrenched in Europe as it has already done in certain parts of the United States, and that 'clients' will believe that a one-hour session with a counsellor is of more value than time spent with a partner, friends and family. Charlton's ultimate conclusion is that counselling is an erroneous profession, and that paid conversationalists are no substitute for real friends.

Personal Responsibility

In counselling clients are expected to accept some measure of personal responsibility for their problems. Therapists also expect clients to unearth past events that may be relevant to their present problems, and to investigate how their largely unconscious behaviour may contribute to these problems. This can be very confusing for clients who are used to attending the medical profession. The Western medical model views patients as 'sick', and expects them to be passive recipients of treatment, with nothing whatever to contribute to their own healing (Smail: 1978).

Landfield (1975) discusses the impact on different clients of the counsellor's 'personal responsibility' theory. "His underprivileged patients learn early that life has limitations. They also learn that treatment for them is largely custodial and medical." Thus, clients who are from a lower class usually only obtain counselling in a public institutional setting. Taking full responsibility for their predicament is reinforced, while there is no mention of social, political, or economic issues in the shaping of each human being. Landfield (1975) goes on to state that "his more privileged clients do learn that professionals will talk with them about their problems. However, they also learn from the pamphlets circulated by associations for mental health that an emotional problem is sickness......for which the person is not responsible." The counsellor's role, therefore, is to convince the client that problems have something to do with their own agency, and that if the link between behaviour and problem can be found, then change can occur. But the first step of this process requires the client to accept at least partial responsibility for his or her problem.

This 'problem' may be anything from a failed relationship, a feeling of disinterest and depression, to the onset of a physical disease, such as cancer. Counsellors postulate that some clients do not want to let go of their symptoms, and hence resist treatment, because they are subconsciously gaining something from the illness or problem (Glasser: 1984). In reality therapy, clients may feel guilty and confused when they are told that the specific problem or illness they have is their responsibility to alleviate.

Value-free Counselling

According to Masson (1988, 294) "no psychotherapy can be value free, and that no psychotherapist can avoid instilling or attempting to instill his or her values in patients." Rosenthal (1955) who carried out research in this area concluded that patients accept the values of their therapists. Hurvitz (1974) stated that psychotherapy creates powerful support for the established order and is anything but value-free. He concluded that psychotherapy challenges, labels, manipulates, rejects or co-opts any person who attempts to change society. Goffman (1961, 366) claims that psychotherapy consists of "holding the sins of the patient up to him and getting him to see the error of his ways."

Empathy and Understanding

One of the cornerstones of counselling is the view that a therapist will be capable of empathising with a client. According to Smail (1978, 118-119), evidence from psychological research into empathy suggests that some people may be consistently more accurate than others in judging what particular people are likely to do or feel in particular situations. However, people who have done well on empathy tests tend not to be people who have particular psychological theories about 'what makes people tick'.

The belief that empathy and understanding is central to all forms of counselling, particularly Rogers' person-centred method, has led to counsellors being trained in empathy. Smail (1978, 119) comments that empathy is not a technical skill that can be learned. Empathy can only occur between people who have a shared world-view and shared experiences, so that understanding and real communication is possible. A further problem with counselling is that a counsellor cannot understand a client by searching through the literature for similar cases. Understanding human behaviour, motivation, thoughts and feelings can only come about by searching within for one's own lived experience (Smail: 1978, 121).

Critical Psychology's View of Mainstream Psychology and Counselling

Critical psychology is an umbrella term that describes a broad number of politically radical responses to, and differences from, mainstream psychology, spanning the Left, feminism, ethnic and anti-racist politics, sexual politics, ecological movements and new forms of spirituality and radical work groups (Centre for Critical Psychology: 1998). Central to critical psychological research and scholarship is the analysis of subjectivity and self-hood, and a recognition of the cultural, political and historical factors which shape experience. Critical psychologists look at issues such as sexuality, gender, ethnicity, disability, social class, power, embodiment, adult and child development, psychotherapy, mental health, pedagogy, spirituality—amongst others. This approach questions accepted truths about subjectivity and experience, and instead acknowledges the importance of the social, cultural, political and economic context in which we live. Research does not take place in a vacuum, nor is this psychology in a laboratory. The research methodologies adopted stand in contrast to the experimental methodologies traditionally used in psychology (Centre for Critical Psychology: 1998).

In critical psychology there is attention to issues of ethics, power, truth, values and ideology in both research and professional practice. In all strands of critical psychology the influence of cultural, political and historical factors that shape experience are acknowledged. This however, is in contrast to many forms of mainstream psychology and counselling which consider themselves to be value free, and so run the risk of bringing ignorance and bias into all research and therapeutic practice. Mainstream psychology and psychotherapy base theories on the study of white middle-class western males, thereby alienating people from different cultures, class, and gender (Centre for Critical Psychology: 1998).

Mental Health as a Form of Social Control

According to Szasz (1961), the whole mental health field is rampant with abuse of power. "Mental illness is a myth whose function is to disguise and thus render more palatable the bitter pill of moral conflicts in human relations" (Szasz: 1961). Szasz argues that there is no such thing as mental illness, although people do have problems coping with life and each other. The fact that certain behaviours are classified as illnesses has serious consequences, Szasz states, such as providing justification for state-sponsored social control. The collaboration between government, and psychiatry or psychotherapy, results in what Szasz calls the "therapeutic state," a system in which disapproved thoughts, emotions, and actions are repressed ("cured") through pseudomedical interventions. Thus illegal drug use, smoking, overeating, gambling, shoplifting, sexual promiscuity, shyness, anxiety, unhappiness, racial bigotry, unconventional religious beliefs, and suicide are all considered diseases or symptoms that need to be cured.

Szasz (1961) states that it is particularly pernicious that the counsellor all too often convinces the gullible patient than he or she is the expert on the patient's life. According to Szasz the whole idea of therapy is crippling due to the authoritarian, top-down stance that is usually adopted by therapists to control and cajole the client into accepting society's status quo.

The Exploitative Nature of Counselling

Dineen (1998) refers to counselling and psychotherapy as "the therapy industry" where psychotherapy now wields all the powerful tools of a successful trade, replete with devious marketing strategies, political support, and a sophisticated "technology of victim-making". According to Dineen (1998), therapists create patients by labelling every quirk of personality a "disorder". Thus, everyone ends up being "abnormal", and the potential market for therapy becomes the whole world.

According to Dryden and Feltham (1994), counselling is a very modern profession, but one which has become a highly lucrative and fashionable career. They state that some counsellors are motivated by humanitarian concerns while others are motivated by less wholesome interests. Feltham (1997) is concerned by the fact that counselling is often a very expensive pursuit for clients, and that some counsellors are reluctant to practice time-limited counselling or brief therapy. American law, insurance and health policies, however, have for some time pushed counsellors into the position of having to justify their work and often to shorten it (Budman and Gurman: 1988).

Carlson (1995) states that one of the most serious criticisms of traditional, long-term relationship-based therapy is that dependency is created, presenting problems are either unaddressed or left unresolved, and clients are often emotionally and financially worse off at the end of counselling than before. Striano (1988) cites many cases of psychotherapy clients she calls 'therapy addicts', who have endured years of unproductive therapy. Due to their own dependency, their wish to please their therapists, and their inability to terminate counselling in the face of their therapists' protestations or manipulations, these people have often forfeited large sums of money, failed to improve, and have in many cases deteriorated. Hopton and Williams (1994: 20) state that counselling organisations' codes of conduct, including the British Association for Counselling and Psychotherarpy, puts no explicit obligations on counsellors to consider the ethics of charging people for counselling.

According to Howard (1996: 176), counsellors are neither better nor worse than the rest of humanity, nor more or less caring or compassionate than anyone else. However, Howard (1996: vii) states that the care professionals are too busy perfecting and packaging their products, and their clients are too preoccupied consuming them, to question whether the amount of expenditure, time and personal investment spent on counselling is ever justified.

Abuse of Power

In "Against Therapy" Masson (1988) describes the very foundation of gestalt therapy to be based on abusive and sexist practices. Masson (1988, 256) quotes Perls, the founder of gestalt, who described an incident in his autobiography that occurred with a female client during a group-therapy session. In "'In and out of the garbage pail" (1969) Perls wrote that, after knocking the woman to the ground three times, "I got her down again and said, gasping: "I've beaten up more than one bitch in my life." Then she got up, threw her arms around me: "Fritz, I love you". Apparently she finally got what, all her life, she was asking for, and there are thousands of women like her in the States. Provoking and tantalising, bitching, irritating their husbands and never getting to their spanking. You don't have to be a Parisian prostitute to need that so as to respect your man".

Masson (1988, 256) states that Perls' attitude to his patients was utterly disrespectful. Masson (1988) quotes Perls from his work "Gestalt Therapy Verbatim" (1969, 57): "A good therapist doesn't listen to the content of the bullshit the patient produces, but to the sound, to the music to the hesitation. Verbal communication is usually a lie." Masson (1988, 257) states that gestalt group therapy depends on one individual who acts as a leader, and that Perls, when he conducted these sessions, encouraged the verbal attacking of individuals by other group members to make them 'get into' their feelings. Masson views this treatment of vulnerable people as a serious abuse of power, and compares it to the behaviour of cult leaders.

Cade and O'Hanlon (1993) in "A brief guide of brief therapy" refer to the potential abuse of power by therapists in directing their clients towards specific goals and behaviours. They also acknowledge that many therapists do not have any awareness of social and political considerations, such as gender and race.

Dineen (1998) discusses the immense damage caused by 'Recovered Memory Therapy', which has led many ordinary people to believe, falsely, that they had been sexually abused as children. She also exposes the cultish nature of the twelve-step program, which presents itself as a single cure-all for every problem imaginable. Dineen states that these are not isolated incidents, and that abuse is endemic in even the most well respected and highly regulated sectors of the therapy industry. For Dineen, the problem with therapy is not just an accident of history for its roots lie buried in the very idea of therapy itself. This is due to the idea that counsellors are "experts in living".

Therapists, according to Dineen, have assumed the position formerly occupied by gurus and priests, pretending they have access to the secret of health and happiness. Dineen (1998) argues that people must regain confidence in their own capacity for self-direction, and realise that therapy is big business, where therapists are more interested in profit than in helping clients.

SUMMARY

This chapter provided a brief review of mainstream counselling theories. Three of the most common forms of counselling—person-centred counselling, gestalt therapy, and reality therapy—are briefly reviewed in terms of their underlying theoretical frameworks. General criticisms of mainstream counselling theories and methods by former counsellors and researchers are then outlined. The issues addressed include research into affects of counselling on clients, the mystique of counselling, contrasting theories and techniques, the artificial nature of the counselling relationship, the counselling cult, personal responsibility, value-free counselling, empathy and understanding, critical psychology's view of mainstream psychology and counselling, mental health as a form of social control, the exploitative nature of counselling, and abuse and power issues.

The next chapter provides a critique of mainstream counselling from a feminist perspective. This investigates the failure of mainstream counselling to address gender stereotypes and power issues within the counselling relationship.

Feminist Counselling

DEFINITIONS OF FEMINIST COUNSELLING

Feminist counselling draws its theories and methods from a variety of diverse sources. There is no definite school of feminist counselling. Most feminist counsellors draw upon many of the techniques of mainstream counselling. At its core however is a form of counselling which is women-centred. Feminist theory rejects the prevailing patriarchal and hierarchical models of control, power and domination (Chaplin: 1992, 3). Feminist therapists use feminism as their doctrine. In this context, feminism means "the freeing of all people from the restrictions of their culturally defined sexual roles and the focus on balancing out the centuries of negation of female energy by the positive assertion and development of it in the world today" (Vesel-Mander and Kent Rush: 1974, 38-39).

Feminist counselling emphasises the interconnectedness between all things and people. According to Chaplin (1992, 3) the feminist counselling model is like a spiral path that goes backwards as well as forwards through many cycles of development and fulfilment. This model allows clients to move between their conscious and unconscious, between their joy and their sorrow, between activity and rest, and between inner and outer worlds.

ROOTS OF FEMINIST COUNSELLING

According to Worell and Remer (1992, 151), the need for feminist counselling emerged from the awareness that assessment and diagnostic approaches used in traditional psychotherapy were susceptible to sex bias in four major areas. These were: disregarding or minimising the affect of the environmental context on individuals' behaviour; different diagnoses being given to women and men who displayed similar symptoms; therapists' misjudgements in the selection of diagnostic labels due to sex-role-stereotyped beliefs; and using a sex-biased theoretical orientation. Feminist counsellors, in contrast to mainstream counsellors, postulate that failure to acknowledge the oppressive societal context in which women live leads many mental health professionals to mislabel women's responses to their environment as pathological (Worell and Remer: 1992, 159). Feminist counsellors (Greenspan, 1983; Sturdivant, 1980) reinterpret women's symptoms and behaviours as being ways of coping in an oppressive, sexist and unequal environment.

Vesel-Mander and Kent-Rush (1974, 13) state that integration is a key word in feminist theory. The roots of feminist counselling lie in the integration of various theoretical and practical disciplines. Vesel-Mander and Kent-Rush (1974, 58) define feminist therapy as "a synthesis of modified traditional therapies and the collective creations and development of the Women's movement". Undoubtedly the Women's movement from the 1960s onwards played a central role in the development of feminist counselling, by the formation of its consciousness raising groups that sought liberation from personal and political oppression. The advent of a new psychology for women, largely heralded by Baker-Miller (1976), challenged much of traditional psychology that assumed male development to be the norm.

There are also other strands of thought that have influenced the feminist counselling model. These include tapping into the ancient myths and symbols of femininity, the writings of feminist psychoanalysts, humanistic psychology, and spirituality and the new age movement with their emphasis on holistic healing (Chaplin: 1992, 10-15). Each of these roots is outlined below.

The Women's Movement

The Women's movement grew out of the struggle for equality and civil rights in the 1960s. Many women became active in striving for political and social reform. In Europe, in Latin America, in China and other Eastern countries, and to a lesser extent in the United States, feminism is linked to Marxist-Leninist ideology (Vesel-Mander and Kent-Rush: 1974, 7). The Women's movement was inspired by the class struggle, and the fight against the capitalist system, which many women saw as the foundation of patriarchy. In the United States, the Civil Rights movement and Gay activists were also supported by various women's groups that campaigned for equality and justice for all.

Running parallel to these political campaigns was an upsurge in feminist writing, including important books by De Beauvoir (1949), Firestone (1949), Millet (1969), Greer (1971), Friedan (1977), Baker-Miller (1976), Daly (1986), and Chodorow (1978). Perhaps the most important factor of all in the success of the Women's movement was the number of groups that formed to raise consciousness among women, and to teach assertiveness and personal development. According to Chaplin (1992, 13) this new sense of empowerment that women began to feel brought with it a desire for further personal work in a safe environment, such as one-to-one counselling.

A New Psychology of Women

Jean Baker-Miller (1976) in "Toward a new psychology of women" challenged traditional psychology for its almost complete ignorance of women's development, sexuality and identity. Traditional psychology split everything into two opposing forces. Being male was associated with all that was strong, assertive, logical and powerful, whereas being female was linked with all that was weak, submissive, emotional and inferior. Women's traditional roles of rearing children, of nurturing and maintaining relationships was denigrated to a lesser realm, compared with the male's active position in the public sphere.

Baker-Miller (1976) wrote of the true importance of being able to share with others and to form and maintain close attachments. "All of living and all of development takes place only within relationships.....women have been assigned to the realms of life concerned with building relationships, especially relationships that foster development. Thus from women's lives we can begin to gain a greater understanding of growth-enhancing interactions. We can see too the obstacles that prevent the full realisation of these interactions. We perceive too the deficiencies and problems in men's development in a new way."

The problems however that many women face by investing heavily in relationships include a loss of investment in themselves and their own growth, a sense of inner emptiness, a lack of self-expression and fulfilment which can lead to depression, suppressed frustration and anger as well as a severe loss of confidence (Baker-Miller: 1976). Women need to become aware of their own needs, to reconnect with their own inner power, creativity and self-esteem, so that ultimately they can feel a deeper psychological contentment (Baker-Miller: 1976).

Worell and Remer (1992, 5) believe that an alternate approach to psychology and counselling for women grew out of their dissatisfaction with existing theories, knowledge base, and treatment approaches. A high proportion of individuals who seek treatment for depression, anxiety, panic, anorexia, phobias and agoraphobia are women. Many of these women were traditionally treated with medication, while the underlying reasons for their distress were never investigated (Worell and Remer: 1992, 6). With the advent of a feminist psychology however, researchers and clinicians are now considering how oversocialisation into passive roles may result in women's over-compliant behaviour, denial of basic needs, and their subsequent susceptibility to anxiety and depression (Worell and Remer: 1992, 50).

Ancient Myths of Femininity

Pre-historical mythology has provided many insights that have been integrated into the development of feminist counselling. Matriarchal goddesses were worshipped as a symbol of the power and mystery of the elements, of the earth and the changing seasons, and of the cycle of life and death. The triple goddess was worshipped as the young maiden (spring) the fertile mother (summer) and the wise old mother (winter) (Chaplin: 1992, 10-12).

Many forms of healing have traditionally been associated with women. In the pre-historic world priestesses seem to have been the most powerful spiritual leaders, healers and guides of their communities (Graves: 1955). In "Dreaming the dark" Starhawk (1990, xxvi) writes of the female tradition of healing, of combining the Goddesses' sacred gift to give and to maintain life with the power to change consciousness, to awaken power-from-within, to bring a feeling of connection with the earth and the spirit realms, to bring health and wholeness. The witches or wise women were "the herbalists, the healers, the counsellors in times of trouble. Their seasonal celebrations established the bond between individuals, the community as a whole, and the land and its resources. That bond, that deep connection, was a source of life—human, plant, animal, and spiritual. Without it, nothing could grow. From the power within that relationship came the ability to heal, to divine the future, to build, to create, to make songs, to birth children, to build culture" (Starhawk (1990).

Psychoanalysis

Freud's theories with regard to female sexuality, namely that young females are envious of the male's penis and also fear that they have been the victims of castration, were challenged by feminist psychoanalysts, including Horney (1924), Brunswick (1928), and Mitchell (1975). Horney (1924) argued that any envy women feel has to do with men's greater power and status in society and has little to do with physical attributes. Other feminists, such as Klein (1932) and Dinnerstein (1978) looked to the first attachment, the mother-daughter relationship, to develop their theories around separation and later love relationships. During the

1970s more and more psychoanalysts began to incorporate feminism into their practice, and a new form of women-centred counselling began to be established.

Although feminist counsellors use many of the insights provided by feminist psychoanalysts to help clients explore their unconscious motivations, they also work with present issues. These include career choices, learning assertiveness techniques, and investigating how to improve material conditions such as housing (Chaplin:1992).

Humanistic Psychology, Spirituality and the New Age Movement

Feminist counsellors were much influenced by the influx of theories in the 1960s, which viewed the human being as a complex integration of body, mind, spirit, intellect, and emotions. These theories included those advocated by humanistic psychology, by eastern philosophies such as Taoism, and new age beliefs in holistic healing (Chaplin: 1992, 15). In the humanistic tradition of counselling, feminist counsellors use techniques from person-centred counselling, gestalt therapy, reality therapy, and many other therapies, including art therapy, inner child work, and bodywork.

FEMINIST COUNSELLING FRAMEWORK

Feminist counsellors utilize basic techniques and methods employed by mainstream counsellors. However there are many areas of divergence in theory and in practice where feminist counsellors are highly critical of mainstream counselling. These criticisms are outlined below.

The Patriarchal Society

In deep contrast to mainstream counselling, feminist counselling is profoundly social and political as well as personal and individual (Chaplin: 1992, 4). The main thrust of feminist counselling is always that women have been victimised for centuries by a patriarchal system, which is deeply oppressive, pervasive and damaging. The feminist approach to counselling incorporates understanding about women's development and mental health arising from women's lower political, social and economic status. Sturdivant (1980) believes that feminist counsellors must have applied feminist principles to their own lives, and to have worked through their own consciousness-raising process. Counselling can then be built on the feminist experience and understanding of the ways in which women's position in society influences their psychological development, their life choices, their relationships and their problems.

The insight of the Women's movement that "the personal is the political" is the main underlying principle of feminist counselling (Lerman: 1976). Individual problems are thus seen to be the result of the social subordination of women as a group i.e. many so-called 'neurotic' patterns which women have developed are seen primarily as survival methods which were adopted in order to cope in an unhealthy society. In feminist counselling, women are helped to identify both the social and personal sources of problems and to look for solutions, which do not involve adjustment to oppressive situations.

Feminist family therapist, Luepnitz (1988), writes of the important part which society and history play in the development of each person's identity within their family of origin. She argues that the patriarchy is very much still part of our lives, as most political, social and religious institutions are dominated by men. The absent father is typical of many families where absence occurs at both a physical and an emotional level. Mothers in many ways have a more difficult time now than in the past as they often work outside of the home, but are also expected to rear children and attend to chores.

Feminist counsellors are aware of these traditional gender and power issues within relationships. They explore gender in the context of society, whereas most schools of family therapy and counselling are inclined to blame mothers either for over-investment or under-investment in their children, and tend not to confront fathers about their lack of support either with housework or child rearing.

Social Responsibility

Unlike mainstream counselling which stresses individual responsibility, feminist counselling emphasises the joint responsibility of individuals and society. According to Vesel-Mander and Kent-Rush (1974, 48) there are several gestalt techniques that may be misused in ways that are contradictory and harmful to feminist consciousness. "One of these is the insistence on the use of "I" instead of "you" or "we" or "they"". Although this technique teaches self-responsibility and self-power, when it is overdone it can deny the influence that people have on each other, and also the affect that interacting with the environment may have. Vesel-Mander and Kent-Rush (1974, 48) argue that even if people change their behaviour, it may not change the response of their environment. Putting all the responsibility on the self may result in a lack of awareness and commitment to the need for social change.

Mainstream counselling also advocates that individuals are in control of their lives. Vesel-Mander and Kent-Rush (1974, 48) stress that "everything is not my projection, and there are many things over which I have little control no matter how clear and sane and together and responsible I become". They feel it is dangerous to tell women that they must take further responsibility, when many of them have been conditioned to take too much responsibility for family and partners. They argue that the roots of many women's problems are in fact social. Vesel-Mander and Kent-Rush (1974, 48) wish to put responsibility back where it belongs "on the oppressive political-economic system".

Unlike feminist therapy, gestalt therapy, according to Vesel-Mander and Kent-Rush (1974, 49) is not focused on inter-relationships but on individualism. "It can be used to heighten personal isolation, discourage communal ties and perpetuate irresponsibility to one another" (1974, 49). This does nothing to foster or nourish relationship, but is a perfect philosophy for a capitalist competitive society and a laissez-faire economic system (1974, 49).

An Egalitarian Relationship

One of the major complaints of the Women's movement with regard to mainstream counselling was that counsellors use their power to coerce women to adapt to an unhealthy environment, and are thus agents of patriarchal control. Feminist counsellor-client relationships minimise the social control aspect of counselling (Worell and Remer: 1992, 94). In feminist counselling the relationship between the counsellor and the client is an egalitarian one (Rawlings & Carter: 1977). The existence of a hierarchical relationship in counselling perpetuates the experience of subordination that is at the very heart of many of women's problems. The feminist counsellor works to create a relationship of equal power, and helps the client to examine objective power relationships in all areas of her life. An awareness of social inequalities is imperative for the feminist counsellor.

According to Chaplin (1992, 22) even the appearance of a counsellor's consultation room—the way it is decorated, its location—all give impressions to the client about the counsellor's class, income, and lifestyle. Likewise with one's dress and one's accent: all these may make a client feel more or less at ease. However, no person is a blank screen. Feminist counsellors wish to be as genuine as possible, expressing openly their beliefs and experiences, yet also exploring issues of feeling 'inferior' and 'superior', 'acceptable' and 'unacceptable', which have been learned from the patriarchal society in which both women have lived.

The emphasis in feminist counselling is for the client to feel empowered. This power is based on a woman's own unique wisdom and inner strength rather than on debasing another person's selfhood. Feminist counselling is based on equality, where differences are acknowledged but also celebrated whenever possible (Chaplin, 1992).

Expertise

Feminist counsellors pay particular attention to the potential for abuse of the power of expertise. They do not assume a superior status because of the expertise they bring to the therapeutic relationship, nor do they allow clients to treat them as superiors (Kaschak: 1981). The client is the real expert on herself and her experience. The counsellor may suggest new ways of looking at and using that experience, but will not offer a diagnosis or give interpretations. Her task is to validate the client's experience, not to analyse it.

Personal validation is often a new experience for many female clients, as is the emphasis on a woman's skills and strengths instead of her weaknesses. Calling people by their first names, using ordinary non-jargon language, creating a holding environment where each person can feel safe and cared about are all-important to feminist counsellors. Also, unlike mainstream counselling, a lot of personal disclosure is frequently made by feminist counsellors when deemed to be appropriate (Kaschak: 1981).

Client-Counsellor Values

It is not possible to have a value-free approach to therapy (Worell and Remer: 1992, 84). Traditional and feminist approaches to counselling differ primarily in the value systems that underlie them. Traditional therapies put an emphasis on therapist objectivity, analytical thinking, therapist expertness and control of procedures, emotional distance from clients, and intrapsychic dynamics (Chaplin: 1992, 84). Sexist traditional therapy ignores the role that client's social, political, economic and cultural environment plays in the problems that clients are experiencing (Chaplin: 1992, 85).

According to Chaplin (1992), counsellor's values influence their work, and those who try to keep them from doing so confuse their clients and may manipulate them with personal beliefs and values presented as facts. The feminist counsellor will therefore make her values explicitly known and encourage her client to do likewise. Often a contract is drawn-up which states the client's goals and the counsellor's contribution required to meet them. This helps both client and counsellor to evaluate whether or not they can work well together to achieve a particular goal (Chaplin: 1992, 85).

Feminist counsellors, although respecting client's values and life choices, will not help a client to pursue certain goals, such as helping a woman to change her lesbian identity, or helping her to fit into a traditional sex-role in order to fulfil the wishes of others (Parry: 1984). Value is placed on being a woman and counselling is concerned with the nature and quality of women's lives. Growth, self-development, consciousness-raising, and sex-role analysis due to the cultural conditioning of women, are usually seen as an important part of feminist counselling (Chaplin: 1992, 85).

Power-Sharing

Feminist counsellors value consensual decision-making, equal access to power and open role options. They are committed to social, institutional, and personal change. They also contend that the accumulation of knowledge has been controlled by a male-hierarchy and the shaping of knowledge has occurred in accordance with male criteria of achievement and performance without regard for the ultimate affects on the quality of life or the nature of reality. Thus the dominant worldview has been shaped by male needs and value patterns which in turn has controlled the definitions of women, of social structures and institutions, as well as thought patterns and the psychic and social processes in society (Ballou and Gabalac: 1985).

Many women who enter counselling have experienced a loss of power in some or all areas of their lives. Abuse of power is what they are familiar with. To many the idea of empowerment is alien. Many women are conditioned to be gentle and passive, and never to challenge the status quo or to stand up for their rights and their basic needs. Feminist counselling seeks to awaken women's own inner power, to help them understand that it is the same power that can either destroy or heal. Feeling power to make choices in ones life is a natural right that each person is entitled to. It is the abuse of power that is never acceptable (Vesel-Mander and Kent-Rush, 1974:, 18-19).

The Expression of Emotion

The counsellor will usually pay particular attention to a cluster of emotional problems that often arise because of the social position of women. Many women are very cut off from their feelings when they first attend counselling. They may feel a deadness or depression. Slowly they may begin to feel angry, helpless, and dependent. The counsellor encourages the full expression of all emotions, from anger, sadness, hurt, rage, and disillusionment, to joy, determination, pride and a sense of fun (Chaplin: 1992).

Worell and Remer (1992, 133) suggest that traditional socialisation has encouraged women to avoid direct confrontation or negative assertion with others. As a consequence of this women are often very self-critical if they feel angry, envious, or have strong feelings of hate towards another. Feminist counsellors need to encourage the appropriate expression of emotion as an important release and a form of empowerment for many women (Chaplin: 1992).

Life Choices

Feminist counsellors support attempts to make life choices which may not be consistent with societal expectations, for example, remaining childfree, choosing non-traditional work, or living in a lesbian relationship. They challenge women's assumptions that they have no alternative but to fit into traditional sex roles. Issues frequently emerge such as financial independence, choices about sexuality, and alternatives to sex-roles in structuring relationships and career (Chaplin: 1992).

The feminist counsellor values the client's assumption of personal power and her ability to make independent decisions, and encourages her to find support from female friends in making changes. Making women aware of community support, and the legal and social groups that are available, is also part of feminist counselling. Rawlings and Carter (1977) point out that it is not sufficient to simply encourage women to develop themselves, they also need support in overcoming the very real barriers to that development.

Counselling Females Exclusively

According to Chaplin (1992, 16), "All feminist counsellors would agree that social structures, such as our limited gender expectations and women's second-class status, affects both our psychology and that of men." Unlike mainstream counsellors, many feminist counsellors choose to work only with women in individual or group situations. Those who also work with men apply the same principles to their work with both sexes but find that different issues arise because of the different positions of men in society (Chaplin: 1992).

Chaplin (1992, 24) stresses the fact that both female counsellor and female client are living in a male dominated society. Even if their life circumstances are different, they have each suffered similar oppression and feelings of inadequacy. Thus the counselling relationship is between two adult women who already share common ground in terms of the experiences endemic to their gender.

Many organisations were set up by feminists in the 1970s, such as the Rape Crisis Centre, to offer support and counselling to women. The Women's Therapy Centre was set up in London in 1976 specifically to treat female clients, regardless of their ability to pay. Special services are offered to women with eating problems, and those who are survivors of sexual abuse or domestic violence (Lawrence: 1997, 2).

The importance of a woman being able to choose a female counsellor is highlighted by Ernst (cited in Lawrance: 1997, 25), as gender plays a major part in the formation of one's identify. Lester (1990) writes that "gender defines and shapes the linguistic and other symbolic structures built during development and, we believe, continues to qualify, largely unconsciously, the psychic reality of everyday life."

According to Lawrence (1997, 8-9), a female client may prefer to see a female therapist because, due to a negative past experience, she has an intense distrust of men, or because she may wish to explore her feelings towards her mother. As the client struggles to define herself through the process of counselling she must, however, learn to assert her separateness from the therapist and from all women.

Support Groups

Counsellors who work with groups of women often feel it allows them to see the commonalties in their experiences, and to discern social causes of what is initially perceived as purely individual problems. Such a group further de-emphasises the power of the counsellor, who encourages group members to support one another and to develop a view of women as both powerful and supportive, and to clarify their own feelings about themselves as women (Parry: 1984, 15-16). Assertiveness training, art therapy, dance, movement and creativity are therapeutic methods often used to promote self-confidence and self-expression. As well as the variety of theories and techniques used by feminist counsellors, many different ideologies are also employed such as socialist, radical, humanistic, 'green', and spiritual (Chaplin: 1992, 17).

Classism and Racism

According to Chaplin (1992, 21) the feminist counsellor is usually more aware of class and racial differences, and the damage to self-esteem that may have been caused by cultural stereotypes, than are most mainstream counsellors. Feminist counselling does not take place in a vacuum, but is embedded in a social and economic context. It acknowledges that counselling is much more accessible for the middle class. For most working class people there usually has to be a serious mental problem before they are liable to seek out counselling.

Chaplin (1992, 24) also emphasises the impossibility of perfectly matching all counsellors and clients with regard to class, race, sexual orientation, lifestyle, and creed. The more that this 'matching' can occur, however, the easier it is for the counsellor to understand the client. Hollingshead and Redlich (1958) found that counsellors' feelings towards clients of their own class were more positive than towards those of different class status.

The feminist counsellor acknowledges the lack of opportunity for personal growth, education, and employment in certain environments or among certain minority groups. Feminist counsellors are also more aware of how their own values may differ from those of non-middle class or ethnically different clients. Class differences are not only economic but also cultural, and deeply affect people's values and lifestyles. Middle-class people and those from western cultures are generally more used to talking about feelings and using phrases that have become part of popular psychology (Chaplin: 1992, 22).

According to Chaplin (1992, 21) mainstream counsellors who are employed by the state may be part of a controlling agency aimed at keeping working-class people in their place. However, feminist counsellors may encourage clients to express their anger at a society that treats them unequally, and may support rebellion and independence. Feminist counsellors tend to work in private practice, since their values would likely clash with institutional agencies that are part of the very patriarchal system which feminists believe to be the reason for much social inequality.

Feminist counsellors are aware of the need to make counselling available to people from non-middle class and minority ethnic groups (Chaplin: 1992, 21). Some of the earliest psychotherapists, such as Adler (1956) and Reich (1970) deliberately chose to work in the poorer areas of Vienna and Berlin, and offered free treatment to clients. Feminist counsellors make the connection between 'personal' and 'political' freedom, and encourage campaigning for political and social change, as well as working with clients to achieve individual growth and insight.

Self-Exploration for Counsellors

Worell and Remer (1992, xvi) stress that effective counselling with women clients requires an awareness of personal stereotypes about women, an understanding of self in relation to women, and a sensitivity to the special psychological and social environments within which women's development takes place. Without such awareness, counsellors are likely to impose their stereotypes on their clients, unwittingly support them in 'adjusting' to the status quo, and in remaining insubordinate life positions (Worell and Remer: 1992, 17-18).

Ernst (cited in Lawrance: 1997, 18) states that it is vital that feminist counsellors acknowledge the existence and affects of transference and counter-transference. Transference is where the client identifies with and projects feelings onto the counsellor. Counter-transference is where the counsellor identifies with and projects feelings onto the client. Ernst states that it is crucial for a feminist counsellor to explore her own biases, and to see the ways in which she may be allowing racist attitudes to pervade her counselling practice. Differences such as colour, creed, class, ethnicity, sexual orientation, age, or disability may bring up strong counter-transference feelings in the counsellor. Unless she is aware of her own exposure to racist stereotypes and cultural bias she will block any feelings of ambivalence, fear or negativity which may be generated when working with a woman who has some different fundamental characteristic from herself (Ernst, cited in Lawrence: 1997, 30-32).

ISSUES ADDRESSED BY FEMINIST COUNSELLORS

Like all counsellors, feminist counsellors address the problems and confusions that are at the heart of the client's current difficulties. However, feminist counsellors seek to help clients grow in awareness as to how their lives have been affected and curtailed by living in a male-dominated society. Hence, many issues that are raised by a client are explored, not only in terms of the woman's personal experiences and relationships, but also in terms of gender stereotypes and power-relations. From how women feel about their bodies, to how women's sexuality is exploited, abused and trivialised, feminist counsellors explore these issues with clients to give them a greater picture of how their own problems, fears, and sense of inferiority are closely entwined with patriarchal values and social constructions.

Sex and Power

Unlike mainstream counsellors, feminist counsellors explore the ways in which sex and relationships are connected to politics. In terms of sex-roles and stereotypes, both socialised sex and politics are both inextricably bound up with power. For millennia, women have been exploited in patriarchal cultures (Vesel-Mander and Kent-Rush: 1974, 22). Worell and Remer (1992, 92) view feminist therapy as focusing on helping clients identify the influence of social rules, sex-role socialisation, institutionalised sexism and other kinds of oppression on personal experience. Feminists of all backgrounds converge on the fact that every area of a woman's life is affected by gender inequalities. Women's bodies and their sexuality is the arena where patriarchal control and violence is most commonly displayed

Women are faced with many opposing images and views of female sexuality. For centuries women were categorised as virgin, mother or whore. Within all major religions female sexuality is viewed as a temptation, leading innocent males towards sin. Patriarchal laws devised ways of controlling female sexuality, making it permissible only within the sanctity of marriage. In Victorian England a woman who enjoyed or pursued sexual pleasure was labelled mentally sick, was often committed to an asylum or was deemed to be in need of a gruesome operation to make her sexually passive, so that she could no longer enjoy sex. Since the 1960s a woman is often deemed to be liberated only if she is having sex with many partners (Worell and Remer (1992).

Feminist counsellors explore these deeply powerful and contradictory stereotypes with clients, teasing out how they have affected women's choices, and the expression of their needs and feelings. According to Vesel-Mander and Kent-Rush (1974, 51), feminism seeks to bring out the validity of the woman's own experience, and to challenge society's artificial norms about what women should and should not want sexually.

Sexual Abuse and Domestic Violence

Many feminist counsellors specialise in working with women who have suffered sexual abuse or violence. Sexual abuse, rape, domestic violence and pornography are crimes that are viewed by feminists as ways in which the patriarchy keeps women frightened and controlled. Feminist counsellors will not only explore the woman's personal experience of abuse but will also look at society's values and stereotypes that create male abusers and female victims.

Women who have been raped may agonise over what it was in their dress or behaviour that precipitated the attack, a question that would be considered ludicrous in any other violent crime. Feminist counsellors work with their clients to help them realise that the crime was in no way instigated by them. Men are overwhelmingly the perpetrators of violence and sexual abuse against women. This violence is not about isolated incidents, but occurs in many contexts, from private and familial, to public (Walsh and Liddy: 1989).

MacLeod (1990, 1) is highly critical of the counselling which women who have suffered domestic violence receive from mainstream counsellors. She states that "mainstream treatment approaches used in social service or health agencies and by private medical, psychological and social work practitioners have been attacked for blaming the woman." She goes on to add that mainstream counsellors often look for weaknesses or pathologies within the woman to explain the violence, minimising or ignoring the responsibility of the violent partner for his actions, and overlooking the social values and institutions that condone violence against women and children. Criticism of mainstream counselling is also made by MacLeod (1990) for its failure to understand the seriousness of the violence and the continued danger many abused women experience, even after separating or divorcing from a violent partner. Also, mainstream counselling often emphasises treatment based on keeping the family together, while failing to recognise the power imbalance that exists between men and women which reinforces abuse (MacLeod, 1990, 2).

Body Image

The way in which women are portrayed in advertising and pornography is also addressed by feminist counsellors. Women are groomed by culture to view themselves as objects, which must match a particular shape and style to fit in with perceived notions of beauty and desire. Despite all the political advances which feminists have achieved over many decades, women still learn to judge their worth by their physical appearance, bodies, faces, hair and clothes (Wolfe: 1991).

Feminist counsellors view such issues as low self-esteem due to poor body image, the use of cosmetic surgery for non-medical treatment, and such problems as bulimia and anorexia nervosa as being largely the result of patriarchal conditioning and exploitation. Psychotherapist, Susie Orbach (1993) explores the reasons why many women become anorexic. In the United States alone, one hundred and fifty thousand women die from the affects of anorexia. For Orbach (1993) the psychological roots of this form of self-inflicted violence are embedded when the woman initially tries to transform her body into that which will be acceptable to society. She surpasses society's demands that a woman be thin and desirable and instead goes on a form of hunger strike, trying to control even her most basic need for food as she has been brought-up to deny her emotional needs.

Feminist counsellors seek to help a woman begin to nurture herself, to learn to love and respect her own body. This helps the woman to grow in self-esteem, and to regain her sense of internal power. Vesel-Mander and Kent-Rush (1974, 56) recommend that feminist counsellors use body therapies because a great deal of women's oppression is biological. As a result of centuries of negative programming, women need to do a great deal of healing on their bodies and body images.

The Female Life Cycle

Worell and Remer (1992, 1) state that "working with women who seek help requires that you are aware of and understand the full context of their experiences and development across the lifespan." Feminist counsellors need to be aware of every aspect of the female life cycle, and of the problems, joys and anxiety which each particular epoch can bring. This awareness, however, encompasses knowledge of cultural conditioning and stereotypes that affect women's expectations as to their role at the various stages of life. The female life cycle involves many separate though integrated stages: birth and childhood, the onset of puberty and menstruation; establishing sexual relationships; leaving home; living alone or with a partner; considering career opportunities; issues around fertility, pregnancy and childbirth; losing friends, family or a partner through separation or death; the menopause; children leaving home; ageing and retirement.

Issues such as PMT (pre-menstrual tension), infertility, abortion, miscarriage, the death of a child, post natal depression, the break-up of relationships, the loss of physical beauty through ageing, and how these deeply affect women may be explored by a feminist counsellor. Patricia Land (cited in Lawrence: 1997, 72) looks at the way ageing specifically affects women. Women have many fears around loneliness, poverty, losing their health and agility, which are similar to men. However women feel very conscious that statistically they are more likely to be left poor and alone than men, and that they face particular health risks, such as osteoporosis and cancer of the breast and uterus. Also many women perceive themselves, and are perceived by others as the carers in families. Many women therefore worry that if they become sick or infirm there will be no one to care for them.

Lesbian Relationships

There are many myths, stereotypes and fears around a woman who chooses to have a sexual or romantic relationship with another woman. She may not be taken seriously, for without a man—a penis—there can be no sexual relationship. Her sexuality may be labelled as perverted or sinful. She may be told she is in need of treatment for some hormonal imbalance. The reality is that some women are quite happy and content to form sexual relationships with women, some are attracted to both men and women and so are open to relationships with both sexes, and others may be attracted to men and never choose to have a sexual relationship with a woman (Dickson: 1989).

One of the central tenets for successful counselling is client-therapist similarity (Guntrip, 1969). It is the therapist's ability to understand intuitively and accurately a particular client that gives the client a feeling of safety and of being understood. Clients who are lesbian have usually suffered the feeling of being alone and different even in their family of origin. Gonsiorek (1985, 23) states that a non-gay therapist only perpetuates the pain of alienation and that it is of vital importance that a person who is lesbian attends therapy with a lesbian therapist. Riddle and Sang (1978) found "a tremendous advantage in having a gay therapist who can model for the client a sense of positive identity."

Feminist counsellors explore issues around a female client being attracted to other women, but also the social and cultural issues. Lesbianism is a great challenge to the very fabric of marriage and patriarchy, and this may be the reason for much fear and outrage against those who are not heterosexual. Many women who are lesbian may have a very difficult time trying to accept their sexuality. Many are frightened to tell parents and friends because they may become isolated and labelled as freaks, and many feel alone and isolated because so many events organised socially are for heterosexual people to meet and form relationships with each other (Dickson: 1989).

The feminist counsellor will work with the woman to help her understand and accept herself, her sexual orientation, her need for fulfilling human relationships with people of her own choosing and for the freedom to express her sexuality in whatever way feels right for her. She may recommend a client to attend a lesbian consciousness-raising support group, or some activity where she can meet others who share her sexual orientation (Dickson: 1989).

SUMMARY

This chapter provided a review of feminist counselling and a critique of main-stream counselling. It explored the roots of feminist counselling, which included the women's movement, a new psychology for women, ancient myths of femininity, psychoanalysis, and humanistic psychology, spirituality and the new age movement. Feminist counselling frameworks were outlined, including the patriarchal society, social responsibility, an equalitarian relationship, expertise, client-counsellor values, power-sharing, the expression of emotion, life choices, counselling females exclusively, support groups, classism and racism, and self-exploration for counsellors. Issues which are frequently addressed by feminist counsellors were also explored, such as sex and power, sexual abuse and domestic violence, body image, the female life cycle, and lesbian relationships.

The next chapter provides a critique of mainstream counselling from a cross-cultural perspective. This looks at the failure of mainstream counselling to acknowledge problems in counselling minority cultures due to the dominance of white western culture in the area of mental health.

Cross-Cultural Counselling

DEFINITIONS OF CULTURE

Culture may be defined broadly to include demographic variables, such as age and gender; status variables, such as social, educational, and economic background; affiliations, either informal or formal; ethnographic variables, such as ethnicity, nationality, language and religion (Pedersen, 1994). A narrow definition of culture is limited to the terms of ethnicity and nationality.

Cross-cultural counselling is the process of counselling individuals who are of a different culture than that of the therapist (Burn, 1992). The concept of culture in counselling usually goes beyond national and ethnic boundaries. It interprets culture in a broader aspect. Culture represents the multiplicity of ways in which human beings adapt to their physical and social environments, and hence culture is of particular importance to counsellors (Das, 1995). Counselling deals with the subjective aspect of culture, such as the internalised feelings, attitudes, opinions and assumptions that members of a particular culture hold.

Herskovits (1948 cited in Serpell 1978) defines culture as the part of the environment which is created or shaped by human beings. Triandis (in Pedersen 1994) focuses on the culture 'in our heads' which is composed of the shared experiences and knowledge of a self-perpetuating and continuous human group, which is part of one's personal reality. Triandis, Bontemplo, Leung & Hui (cited in Pedersen 1996) distinguished between demographic, cultural and personal constructs. They identified cultural constructs as being shared by a group of people who live in the same geographical location at the same time, who speak the same dialect and who share the same norms, roles, values, and ways of describing experience. Multiculturalism seems to capture together the unique interaction among many different variables that together form cultural diversity.

Philips and Rathwell (1986) state that the study of culture and race has more to do with social relationships, power and domination than with biological differences. Dominelli (1988) declares that racism is about the construction of social relationships on the basis of an assumed inferiority of ethnic minority groups and, following on from this, their exploitation and oppression.

Fernando (1988) observes that in psychiatry, culture and ethnicity have political connotations. Fernando (1988) states that culture is used in psychiatry in an ethnocentric way. Consequently, non-western cultures that are alien to psychiatry and psychology are seen as pathological. Hence, culture is seen as the problem that accounts for the 'abnormal' behaviour of the client.

DIVERSITY OF CULTURE WORLDWIDE

Increasingly, counsellors in the western world are called upon to work with clients from different cultures, social class, religion, and ethnicities. In the United States, for example, ethnocultural groups include White Anglo-Saxons, White ethnics, Socioreligious ethnics, Blacks, Hispanics, Asians, and Native Americans. Likewise in Ireland, with the migration of people throughout the European Union, and the arrival of refugees and asylum seekers, a new pluralistic society has been created. Old models derived from mainstream counselling, which largely ignore any mention of cultural diversity or social difference, can offer little to those clients from different cultures who seek counselling.

According to Sue and Sue (1981) the complexity of worldviews creates both problems and opportunities for counsellors. A new multicultural framework of assessment and treatment must be developed for such a diverse population. Counsellors are required to adjust and adapt approaches in developing credibility, empathy, analysis, and communication with each culturally different client. An additional problem for the counsellor is that of cultural self-awareness. Understanding one's own culture and the affect it has on both the client and the counsellor presents an opportunity for self-discovery, growth and creative intervention in the counselling session. Investigating other cultures and learning to respect other ways of feeling, thinking and living, are all crucial if cross-cultural counselling is going to succeed at any level (Sue and Sue: 1981).

THE MANY PERSPECTIVES USED IN COUNSELLING THE CULTURALLY DIFFERENT

There are different perspectives and techniques used in counselling the culturally different which put stress on various aspects of culture. Some perspectives regard culture as a separate entity from demographic factors. In most of the counselling literature, culture is generally synonymous with race and ethnicity. Other possible cultural dimensions, such as religion, gender, or social class are usually ignored. Dimensions, such as disability, sexual orientation and age are often addressed apart from culture.

In the area of counselling, there are three different types of responses to cross-cultural counselling. According to Berry (1969) counsellors should start with training, experience and the sensitivity they have accumulated with their within-cultural clientele, and then they may extend and modify their interventions in culturally different counselling encounters. The second outlook is for the counsellor to undertake a careful conceptual analysis of a culture's values and practices, including its therapeutic interventions, and eventually incorporate these components into modern counselling techniques. In the third approach the counsellor identifies cultural obstacles to effective and helpful intervention. Once the barriers are identified, they can be removed and a culturally appropriate solution may be proposed.

None of these techniques, however, recognises culture as being a different dimension with its own rules and values. Each technique fails to consider the difficulties that may be encountered in defining and stating cultural boundaries as well as removing them. Cultural awareness in this case is helpful, but the fact that cultural differences are sometimes hard to distinguish from demographic or personal characteristics makes it difficult to accurately identify them.

Egan (1998) shows a counselling model that regards cultural differences in the context of assumptions, beliefs, and norms. He claims that in order for a counsellor to be efficient, he or she should understand the different needs and practices inherent in a particular culture. Also the counsellor must understand the specific nuances related to demographic factors, and must respect that behind their shared humanity, clients differ from one another in many aspects.

THE EXCLUSION OF CULTURE FROM MAINSTREAM COUNSELLING

According to Sue and Sue (1981, 4) most graduate mainstream counselling courses fail to cover the major issue of counselling the culturally different client. McFadden and Wilson (1977) report that less than 1% of the respondents in a survey of counsellor education programs reported instructional requirements for the study of non-white cultures. As a result of this lack of training, whenever professionals are dealing with mental health problems of ethnic minorities, they lack the understanding and knowledge about ethnic values and the problems of racism in society.

Counsellor education programs have been accused of fostering western culture, and of completely ignoring other cultures. According to Sue and Sue, (1981, 5) mainstream counselling education:

1. substitutes model stereotypes for the real world

2. disregards cultural variation in a dogmatic adherence to some universal notion of truth

3. uses a technique-orientated definition of the counselling process.

This results in the counsellor's role being rigidly defined, and definitions of normality being equated with the dominant culture's values and beliefs. The label 'mental illness' has traditionally been used as a political tool to control, brainwash or reorient identified victims to fit in with accepted social norms (Thomas and Silken: 1972). Abnormality today is still equated with those traits or attributes which occur least frequently in society, or which are least desirable. The behaviour of individuals belonging to ethnic minorities is often considered to be abnormal and in need of treatment (Sue and Sue: 1981).

Many minorities are suspicious of western mental health professionals, including counsellors, because they feel their values and lifestyles are viewed by society as pathological. Thus they feel discriminated against by a mental health system that is based on the values and characteristics of white middle-class theories and methods (Sue and Sue: 1981).

According to Agoro (2003), counsellors and clients are unlikely to see themselves in a racial or cultural way. There is a serious lack of awareness that the values and practices prevalent in a white British culture, for example, are not universal, and do not constitute the norm. Agoro states that there are several key characteristics that distinguish anti-racist counselling practices from other counselling approaches. These include an understanding and analysis of racism, an active commitment to eradicate racism and to respect diversity of other cultures, a commitment to facilitate cultural sensitivities, and an awareness of counsellors' own cultural beliefs and practices.

PROBLEMS IN COUNSELLING CULTURALLY-DIFFERENT CLIENTS

The various problems in counselling culturally-different clients as highlighted by current research are outlined below.

Values Antagonistic to Third World Clients

It has been asserted by some researchers that the values of counselling may be antagonistic to the values of third world clients. Counselling and psychotherapy have traditionally been conceptualised in western individualistic terms (Atkinson et al, 1989). This seems to be true whether the particular theory is psychodynamic, existential-humanistic or behavioural in orientation. A number of individuals (Ivey, Bradford-Ivey, and Simek-Downing, 1996; Katz, 1985) indicate that these theories share certain common components of white culture in their values and beliefs. Generic characteristics of counselling can be seen to fall into three major categories as put forward by Sue and Sue (1981):

1. Culture-bound values: individual centred, verbal, emotional, and behavioural communication pattern from client to counsellor; openness and intimacy, analytical, linear and verbal approach, with clear distinctions between mental and physical well being.

2. Class-bound values: strict adherence to time-schedules (50 minute, once a week meeting), ambiguous or unstructured approach to problems, and seeking long-range goals or solutions.

3. Language variables: use of standard English and emphasis on verbal communication.

Mainstream counselling appears to be so closely bound up with western culture that its value to clients from other cultures must be seriously questioned. Indeed, further research is urgently needed to ascertain the emotional and psychological damage that may be inflicted on some culturally-different clients who are subjected to western-based counselling.

Ethnic Similarity of Client and Counsellor

Calia (1966) found perceived similarity between counsellor and client to be positively correlated with unconditional regard and empathy, and to be vital for effective growth-promoting relationships. Sue and Sue (1981, 69) state that a counsellor of dissimilar ethnicity may not be able to induce change in a client. They conclude that at times racial dissimilarity may prove to be so much of a hindrance that counselling is rendered ineffective.

According to Jones (1978), the majority of studies conducted on the importance of ethnic similarity between client and counsellor indicate that blacks respond more favourably to black counsellors. His investigations revealed that "blacks prefer black counsellors, achieve greater rapport and engage in greater self-exploration, and are better understood by black counsellors than white". Jones (1978) concluded that attending a counsellor who was of a similar race was of more importance than counsellor experience for the success of black clients in counselling.

According to Mohamed and Smith (cited by Laurence, 1997, 135) white counsellors are less aware of the problems facing black people living in a predominantly white society. Black people living in Britain face many social disadvantages, such as poverty, inadequate housing, unemployment or low-status work, and poor educational opportunities. Certain psychological trends are also apparent, such as the experience of racial discrimination that often leads to depression, anxiety and low self-esteem.

Markowitz (1994) studied the practices of a therapeutic group in New Zealand. He concluded that this group believed that therapeutic conversations across cultural lines were inherently problematic. In their view, no outsider could overcome cultural biases and, therefore, would never be able to accurately judge another culture's understanding of what constitutes normal or abnormal, healthy or unhealthy behaviour.

Individual-Centred Counselling

Most forms of counselling and psychotherapy tend to be individual centred. Pedersen (1987) notes that U.S. culture and society is based upon the concept of individualism, and that competition between individuals for status, recognition, and achievement forms the basis for western tradition. He notes that not all cultures view individualism as a positive orientation; rather it may be perceived in some cultures as a handicap to attaining enlightenment, one that may divert people from important spiritual goals.

In many non-western cultures, identity is viewed as being synonymous with group orientation. The personal pronoun 'I' in the Japanese language does not seem to exist. The notion of 'atman' among Hindus defines itself as participating in unity with all things and not limited by the temporal world. Many societies do not define the psychosocial unit of operation as the individual. In many cultures and subgroups, the psychosocial unit of operation seems to be the family, group or collective society (Puniamurthy: 2000).

In Malaysian society, one's identity is generally defined within the family constellation. The greatest punishment is for a person to be disowned. This happens, for instance, when one marries someone in spite of parental objection or commits an act that brings dishonour to the family. What this means in essence, is that the person no longer has an identity (Puniamurthy: 2000).

Verbal and Behavioural Expression

According to Puniamurthy (2000) many counsellors tend to emphasise the importance of verbal expression. It is preferred that clients are verbal, articulate and are able to express their thoughts and feelings clearly. Individuals are encouraged to get in touch with their feelings and to be able to verbalise their emotional reactions. In some counselling approaches, it is stated that if a feeling is not verbalised and expressed by the client, it may not exist. Behavioural expressiveness is also valued and believed to be important.

These characteristics of counselling can place culturally-different clients at a major disadvantage. Malaysians, for example, tend not to value verbalisations as westerners do. Traditionally, children are taught not to speak until spoken to. Patterns of communication tend to be vertical, flowing from those who are older or of higher status to those who are younger or of lower status. Emotional expressiveness seems not to be desired especially among Malaysian males who value restraint of strong feelings. Malaysian culture emphasises that maturity is associated with one's ability to control emotions and feelings. Thus, culturally insensitive counsellors may perceive such behaviour in a negative psychological light (Puniamurthy: 2000).

Psychotherapy rarely appears to be offered as a form of treatment to black people, because mental health professionals see black people as lacking the necessary verbal skills to articulate their distress. Instead, physical treatments such as medication or ECT[6] are more likely to be proscribed (Mohamed and Smith, cited by Laurence, 1997, 145).

Insights

It is assumed to be mentally beneficial for individuals to obtain insight or understanding into the causes of apparent problems. Many theorists, especially from psychoanalytical schools of thought, tend to believe that clients who obtain insight into their problems will be better adjusted in society (Puniamurthy: 2000).

Insight is not valued by many culturally-different clients, however, especially those from lower socio-economic groups. Their main concern is how to survive on a day-to-day basis rather than to be involved in insightful processes. Malaysian Chinese, in particular, believe that thinking too much about something can cause problems and therefore discourage self-exploration. Instead, they are advised to keep themselves busy and not to dwell on their problems. Thus a counsellor who is seeing a Malaysian Chinese client, and who has no awareness of this client's reluctance to partake in a search for insight into problems, will probably find very little success with the traditional counselling process (Puniamurthy: 2000).

Self-Disclosure

In counselling, one's ability to self-disclose and to talk about the most private aspects of one's life is much valued. This is not acceptable to most Malaysians as revelations of personal and social problems reflect, not only on the individual, but on the whole family (Puniamurthy: 2000). Thus, the family may exert strong pressure on the client not to reveal personal matters to outsiders. In this situation, a counsellor may wrongly perceive that the client is repressed, inhibited, shy, passive or uncooperative.

Ambiguity

The ambiguous and unstructured aspect of the counselling situation, especially in the person-centred approach, may create discomfort and confusion in Malaysian clients. They may not be familiar with counselling and may perceive it as an unknown and mystifying process (Puniamurthy: 2000).

Communication Patterns

A significant area in communication is the non-verbal component (Wieman and Harrison, 1983: Wolfgang, 1985). This refers to facial expression, posture, movement, gestures, and eye contact. Interpreting non-verbal communication, however, is rather difficult for counsellors for several reasons. Firstly, non-verbal behaviour varies from one cultural group to another. Secondly, it is often outside our level of awareness. Consequently, it is important that counsellors recognise non-verbal communications and their possible cultural meanings.

Much of counselling assessments is based upon expressions on people's faces (J.C. Pearson, 1985). It is assumed that facial cues express emotions and demonstrate the degree of responsiveness and involvement of the individual. However Asian people, such as the Chinese, restrain strong feelings like anger and happiness, and this is considered to be a sign of maturity and wisdom. Counsellors may assume that their Asian client is lacking in feelings or is not willing to take part in the counselling process. Malaysian Indians tend to nod and use a lot of hand gestures during a conversation, which makes it difficult to interpret their meaning (Puniamurthy: 2000).

Eye contact is the non-verbal behaviour most likely to be addressed by counsellors in the belief that eye contact or lack of eye contact has diagnostic significance. In most cases, counsellors attribute negative traits to the avoidance of eye contact. In the Malaysian context, direct eye contact is avoided or kept to a minimum between members of the opposite sex. This is very prevalent in Muslim society where some women even cover their faces to signify modesty (Puniamurthy: 2000).

Shaking hands also varies from culture to culture. Malaysians use both hands gently to shake among members of the same sex. Any form of physical contact between members of a different sex is frowned upon. In Asian society, touching anyone with the left hand may be considered an obscenity, as the left hand is an aid to the process of elimination (Puniamurthy: 2000). All of these customs may cause great misunderstanding and may even sabotage the entire counselling process if a counsellor is not aware of the meaning ascribed to non-verbal cues by culturally different clients.

Language

Western society is monolingual and places a high premium on the use of English. Studies indicate that simply coming from a background where one or both parents have spoken their native tongue can impair proper acquisition of English. Marcos et al (1973) report that if bilingual individuals do not use their native tongue in counselling, many aspects of their emotional experience may not be available for discussion or treatment.

Paralanguage

This term refers to other vocal cues that are used to communicate such as loudness of voice, pauses, silence, hesitations, and inflections. It can communicate a variety of different features about a person, such as age, gender and emotional responses as well as the race and sex of the speaker (Mehrabian, 1972).

Americans frequently feel uncomfortable with a pause or silent stretch in the conversation, feeling obligated to fill it in with more talk. In Malaysian culture, silence is traditionally a sign of respect for their elders. Often, silence is a sign of politeness and respect rather than a lack of desire to continue speaking. A counsellor who misinterprets silence may fill in the conversation and prevent the client from elaborating further. Thus, it can be seen how counselling, which emphasises verbal expression, may place many minorities at a disadvantage (Puniamurthy: 2000).

Directness of a conversation also varies considerably among various cultural groups. Westerners tend to get to the point without going around in circles. In contrast, Asians take great care not to embarrass the other person by using euphemisms and being ambiguous (Puniamurthy: 2000).

Class-Bound Values

For the counsellor who generally comes from a middle or upper class background, it is often difficult to relate to the circumstances and problems affecting the client who lives in poverty. Lewis (1966) describes the phenomenon of poverty and its affects on individuals and institutions. The client's life may be characterised by low wages, unemployment, little or no property ownership, no savings and lack of food reserves. There may be a constant struggle to meet even the basic needs of hunger and shelter. Counsellors may attribute attitudes that result from physical and environmental factors to the cultural or individual traits of the person.

Due to the client's underprivileged environment, and past inexperience with counselling, the expectations of the client may be quite confused or negative.

Thus, the client may be perceived by the counsellor to be hostile and resistant (Puniamurthy: 2000).

Stereotyping

Although it is crucial for counsellors to have a basic understanding of counselling characteristics and value systems of culturally different clients, there is the danger of overgeneralisation and simplification. The general characteristics of an ethnic group do not indicate that all persons coming from a minority group will share all or some of these traits. It is highly improbable that one can enter a situation or deal with people without forming impressions consistent with one's own experiences and values. Generalisations are useful, serving as guidelines for our behaviour, especially in new situations, but they should be open to change and challenge (Sue and Sue 1999).

However, when generalisations become stereotypes the client cannot be seen clearly by the counsellor. Stereotypes may be defined as rigid preconceptions we hold about all people who are members of a particular group, whether it be defined along racial, religious, sexual or other lines (Sue and Sue: 1999). The belief in a perceived characteristic of a group is applied to all members without regard for individual variations. The danger of stereotypes is that they are imperious to logic or experience. Malaysians, for example, are perceived as very gentle and leisure-loving people, while the Chinese are considered to be hard working and an economically motivated group. These generalisations may be true to some extent but stereotyping can lead to misunderstanding and prejudices (Puniamurthy: 2000).

It is also likely that clients from different cultures may hold stereotypical views that may be applied to the counsellor from the dominant culture. Feelings of mistrust are often experienced by clients for their culturally-different counsellors (Deloria, 1983). The counsellor can avoid the hasty perception that client hesitation, steeped in mistrust, is indicative of denial and resistance to treatment.

The Failure of Mainstream Counselling to Work Effectively with Culturally Different Clients

According to Chapman (1988), mainstream-counselling literature has been dominated by articles concerning the theory and the application of techniques in the treatment of clients with various addictions. Such theories have been primarily postulated by a white middle class counselling establishment, as is the case with most literature on psychotherapy (Pedersen, 1987). To this end, culturally different clients have not fared well with such approaches to counselling in general (Sue and Sue: 1981) and addiction counselling specifically.

From the early 1960's reports began to emerge of the counselling profession's failure to adequately serve those from non-western cultures. The lack of cultural sensitivity in counselling included the mistaken belief that counselling is the preferred mode of intervention to assist individuals in all cases of maladaptive behaviour. Recently, the western counsellor has begun to realise that counselling and psychotherapy are merely representative of the many approaches to providing mental health services worldwide (Pedersen, 1987).

The counsellor's perception of client progress in treatment is often influenced by that counsellor's cultural perspective or bias. When addressing addiction problems, with their high incidence of denial and low levels of commitment to abstinence, the issue of cultural bias becomes significant when evaluating the treatment needs and progress of the culturally different client (Chapman: 1988).

Stereotypical Views Held by the Counsellor

The counsellors' dogmatic acceptance of the stereotypical beliefs of the dominant culture promotes a view that the resolution of problems in treatment for the non-western client is the client's responsibility. An example of this is where a mainstream counsellor expects a client to be prompt for each session. Due to culturally based differences in the value placed on promptness, a client may be consistently late for scheduled appointments. This behaviour may be misinterpreted by the counsellor as the client's unwillingness to attend counselling. In actuality, such tardiness is frequently experienced when treating Native Americans who hold strong beliefs regarding the importance of the temporal present and a commitment to such values (Richardson, 1981). Consistent tardiness is often misinterpreted by the counsellor who is unfamiliar with culturally-based perceptions of time (Chapman, 1988).

Insensitivity to Cultural Variations

Cultural bias certainly adds to the counsellor's difficulty in establishing a relationship with a culturally different client. It also significantly increases the likelihood that a misperception of denial or a lack of commitment to treatment will result in an ineffective or unnecessary intervention. The client usually assumes that the mainsteram counsellor is unfamiliar with the client's culture (Deloria,1983). Many professionals fail to learn about the various cultural values of their client and are unaware of the importance of counsellor sensitivity to the issues of counselling across cultures. This usually results in one or more of the following:

1. A general lack of understanding of the client's native culture

2. Counsellor retention of stereotypical cultural views of the client

3. The use of standardised techniques and approaches to treatment with all clients, regardless of their cultural background (Chapman, 1988).

On those occasions where a clinician works or lives close to the environment from which the culturally different client resides, it can be both helpful and enlightening to become familiar with the client's culture. These exposures to the values and customs of other ethic groups result in a better appreciation for and sensitivity to the issues affecting the lives of clients being treated (Chapman, 1988). The counselling process is also aided when the counsellor shows a respect for the culture of his or her client. Lewis and Ho (1975), in referring to Native Americans, suggest that a counsellor who shows respect for the system, values, and norms of the client eventually places him or herself in a position of trust and credibility.

Counsellor Perceives Resistance to Treatment

The acceptance of stereotypical assumptions about counselling, its outcome, and appropriate client responses increase the likelihood that the counsellor will perceive a resistance to treatment when therapeutic suggestions are resisted by the client. A classic example is when the culturally insensitive counsellor encounters a Native American client. Being unfamiliar with the traditional Native American value of maintaining a posture of non-involvement, and avoiding behaviour that could be construed as attention seeking, the counsellor perceives resistance to treatment in the behaviour of the client who refrains from active participation in group or individual counselling (Richardson, 1981; Trimble, 1981).

Power Issues

According to Sue and Sue (1981, 69) clients who are culturally different from the counsellor may not be as impressed with the counsellor's qualifications or perceived expertness. Clients from minority groups may be particularly sensitive to racism and may judge the effectiveness of the counsellor upon his or her knowledge of ethnic issues. Tests of credibility and trustworthiness may occur frequently during counselling, so that the counsellor's power base may be constantly threatened. This may feel very uncomfortable for the counsellor who is not used to being challenged. In this case the counsellor may become excessively defensive and may challenge the client for being uncooperative, thereby causing the client to terminate therapy.

Clinical Arrogance

Clinical arrogance attributes all problems in therapy to the client. A counsellor who feels excessively challenged and who misrepresents a client's intentions, may make recommendations that will negatively affect the client. Examples of such measures in the US where counselling has been requested by a court of law, may include the termination of social service benefits, a recommendation of incarceration, termination of employment, or the placement of the client's children in foster care. Confrontation is an effective tool in addressing genuine resistance to treatment. However, if a client's behaviour is culturally motivated rather than genuine denial, the confrontation only serves to reinforce the client's perception of institutional racism (Chapman, 1988).

MODELS USED IN CROSS-CULTURAL COUNSELLING

Two models used to counsel culturally different clients that address some of the problems highlighted so far in this chapter are outlined below.

Three-Dimensional Model for Counselling Ethnic Minorities

A particularly useful model for counselling culturally different clients is the one proposed by Atkinson, Thompson and Grant (1993). In this model, three factors need to be taken into account when a counsellor selects his or her role and strategies for working with ethnic minorities. These are:

1. Client's level of acculturation

2. Locus of etiology[7]

3. Goals of helping.

Acculturation refers to the extent to which an individual has adopted the beliefs, values, customs and institutions of the dominant culture. The causes of problems that clients bring to counselling can be conceptualised as ranging from an internal source to an external one. Goals of counselling can be conceptualised as ranging from prevention of problems to solution of problems. Goals of counselling often include both preventative and remediative measures, and can be conceptualised somewhere between the two extremes.

Counsellors need to function as advocates for clients who are low in acculturation and who need a solution to a problem that results from oppression and discrimination. Clients who are new to a culture may manifest some intrapersonal and interpersonal problems that have an internal source or at least that are not directly the result of discrimination and oppression. In order to help these clients, a counsellor needs to know the kind of support systems available in the indigenous culture. One way for a counsellor to act as a facilitator is by referring a client to a healer from his or her own culture. For example, a Chinese client could be directed to attend an acupuncturist. Another method is direct application of these traditional systems if the counsellor is trained in such healing methods (Puniamurthy: 2000).

A Sociodynamic Perspective for Counselling

By the late 1970's Peavy (1977, 1979, 1988) had become quite dissatisfied with most existing models of mainstream counselling. He cited three main reasons for the failure of mainstream counselling to successfully treat clients:

1. Nearly all counselling and therapy models were based on positivist premises and suffered from reductionism and fragmentation

2. The professionalisation of counsellors and their elevation to expert-status all too often resulted in their alienation from help-seekers, especially those who come from a lower socioeconomic class, and those who are culturally different, or poorly educated

3. Psychology, especially abnormal psychology with the accompanying vocabularies of pathology and deficiency, remain dominant in the thinking of counsellors. Too often, counsellors as well as psychologists and teachers try to explain and analyse what is going on from the perspective of a "disturbed" or "deficient" individual. Socio-cultural contexts are largely ignored by mainstream counselling.

Peavy (1977) founded the Sociodynamic school of counselling. He claimed that this method of counselling was not an expert oriented procedure in which the counsellor is alienated from the client by virtue of status and vocabulary. Instead he viewed counselling as a process where both people could contribute to finding creative solutions to the client's life situation. This counselling method stresses the importance of the social environment, and focuses on aiding clients to participate more fully in daily sociocultural life. This perspective is in sharp contrast to mainstream counselling which seeks to change people's behaviour and cognition.

Peavy (1977) encountered widespread resistance to his ideas from other academics. The notion that counselling should be moved from a psychological base to a multi-disciplinary or social base, and from scientific pretensions to cultural knowledge, was too drastic and revisionary for most of his colleagues. What Peavy envisioned was a counselling technique which facilitated 'help seekers' to perform more successfully and to find meaning in everyday living, such as in their working life, relationships, and family life.

SUMMARY

This chapter provided a review of cross-cultural counselling and a critique of mainstream counselling from a cross-cultural counselling perspective. Problems identified in counselling individuals from different cultures are addressed. These include values antagonistic to third world clients, ethnic similarity of counsellor and client, individual centred counselling, verbal and behavioural expression, insights, self-disclosure, ambiguity, communication patterns, language, paralanguage, class-bound values, and stereotyping. The failure of mainstream counselling to work effectively with culturally different clients was also explored. This addresses such issues as stereotypical views held by counsellors, insensitivity to cultural variations, counsellor's perception of resistance to treatment, power issues, and clinical arrogance. New models used in cross-cultural counselling are also outlined, such as the three-dimensional model for counselling ethnic minorities, and a sociodynamic perspective for counselling.

The next chapter provides a critique of mainstream counselling from a liberation psychology perspective. It addresses the failure of mainstream counselling to acknowledge the need for social change as well as for personal change.

Liberation Psychology

ROOTS OF LIBERATION PSYCHOLOGY

Liberation psychology provides an analysis of the psychological damage associated with oppression. It aims to develop practices that will transform negative psychological patterns, and facilitate taking action to bring about social change (Moane: 1999, 1). Those who write about and practice liberation psychology draw on psychology, feminism, liberation theology, emancipatory education, socialism, and writings on colonialism.

According to Ruth (1988, 443), "whether we are dealing with Irish liberation, or women's liberation, or men's liberation, or travellers' liberation, the key steps are clarifying and interrupting the workings of internalised oppression, developing a clear policy for achieving liberation uninfluenced by internalised oppression, and reaching out to others to win their support for this policy." Liberation psychologists focus on the impact of oppressive social conditions, such as violence, torture, poverty and racism on psychological functioning, ranging from self and identity to creativity and spirituality. Liberation psychologists desire not only to empower individuals trapped in unhealthy and inhumane environments but also to resist oppression and to bring about social change through political and social reform. Liberation psychology is context specific and is grounded in real lived experiences of social injustice, oppression and liberation (Moane: 1999, 1).

Since liberation psychology is context specific, the processes and practices to facilitate liberation may vary from one context to another. A liberation psychology for lesbians and gays may differ from one that seeks the liberation of Argentineans from a dictatorial government. However, a fundamental assumption of all liberation psychologists is that psychological patterns are related to the social conditions in which people live their lives. Thus, the focus is on power inequalities and the psychological affects, such as depression, fear, anger, drug use or hopelessness, which form part of people's experiences in hostile environments. This is in contrast to traditional psychology and mainstream counselling which concentrate on family of origin as the source of psychological distress (Moane: 1999, 2).

LIBERATION PSYCHOLOGY FRAMEWORK

A liberation psychology produces a clear social analysis wherever it encounters oppression. This analysis provides an understanding of the psychological patterns associated with oppression. Three levels of analysis that are usually employed have been identified by Moane (1999, 4). These are:

1. Macro level analysis of social structures and ideology

2. Intermediate level analysis of the community or organisation

3. Micro level analysis of the immediate environment of particular individuals.

At the macro level, patterns of oppression usually include all levels of violence, political exclusion, economic exploitation, sexual exploitation, control of culture and fragmentation. At the intermediate level, patterns of oppression include organisational hierarchies, lack of resources, and instability. At the micro level, patterns of oppression include assaults, non-verbal behaviour, bullying and sexual harassment. This framework shows that there are enormous social forces operating to produce considerable psychological pressures for those experiencing oppressive social conditions. These forces impact heavily on the day-to-day life of the oppressed society, the various communities, and the individuals who live there.

Oppression at the personal level has been identified by liberation psychologists to manifest in various ways (Moane: 1999, 4). This includes feelings of tension and ambivalence in many areas such as sexuality, spirituality and creativity; loss of identity and splits within the self; a sense of inferiority, lack of self worth and self doubt; a variety of negative emotions such as fear, hopelessness, anger and shame; difficulties in relationships such as distrust, misplaced anger, and problems in communication. Mainstream counselling all too often attributes these symptoms as being caused by individual trauma, instead of looking at social issues of inequality and oppression, and how these affect feeling, thinking and behaviour.

Change is viewed by liberation psychologists to take place in relationships and within communities, which begin to become aware of social oppression and injustice. The women's liberation movement and the gay liberation movement are examples of oppressed people bonding together in a common cause. According to Moane (1999, 5) the initial experience of joining a group brings an awareness of lack of confidence, which leads to an interest in personal development, such as assertiveness training. Being part of a group also raises awareness about the ways in which individuals are oppressed, giving members a sense of solidarity and a feeling of support and empowerment. Negative stereotypes of inferiority and social norms are exposed and disempowered. This may eventually lead to an interest in social change and political campaigning. Liberation psychology is a process involving a gradual growth in awareness, building strengths, making connections, and taking action (Moane: 1999, 5). This system of individual and social change occurring simultaneously in groups comprised of like-minded peers is very different from the hierarchical client-counsellor model that is all but oblivious to the need for social change.

LIBERATION PSYCHOLOGY AND COUNSELLING

An analysis of the psychological damage inflicted due to oppression can be applied in a community context or in the context of counselling and psychotherapy. Liberation psychology is particularly relevant to nations that have been colonised. In the Irish context, writers have used liberation psychology to offer greater understanding of the legacies of colonialism and the impact of conflict. Elements of liberation psychology have also been incorporated into many social movements, including the women's liberation movement in Ireland (Moane: 1999, 1). In South America, psychotherapists have used liberation psychology to work with those who have suffered a great deal of trauma and oppression, including dispossession and control of culture.

KEY ISSUES ADDRESSED BY LIBERATION PSYCHOLOGY

There are several key issues that are of particular concern to liberation psychologists. These issues centre on the need for social change, the acknowledgement of social inequalities and injustices, and the moving away from a preoccupation with the self. Liberation psychology advocates an appreciation of difference and a reconciliation of perceived opposites, such as among people of different gender, colour, creed, or culture. There is also a rejection of any form of psychotherapy or psychology that insists upon neutrality in a clearly oppressive or violent situation. Each of these issues is dealt with in more detail below.

The Need for Social Change

The approach of liberation psychologists who practice counselling is in sharp contrast to mainstream counsellors. Mainstream counsellors tend to focus on personal change as the means of becoming psychologically whole. Moane (1999, 17) in "Gender and Colonialism: A Psychological Analysis of Oppression and Liberation", states that Rogers and other theorists involved in the human potential movement did not pay attention to the ways in which the social context would foster or inhibit psychological growth and development. Rogers' interest was firmly focused on the individual and his or her personal experiences, whereas the role of social conditions in creating psychological distress was ignored.

Liberation psychologists strongly reject the notion of personal change without also attending to the need for social change. Liberation psychologists advocate that living in oppressive social conditions is the source of an individual's inability to function in that society. Thus for liberation psychologists, personal change, social change and political change are all part of the process of personal healing, growth and liberation (Moane: 1999, 2).

Alsup (2000) worked as a psychologist for over twenty-one years with Native Americans. Alsup concluded that the discipline of psychology needed to be liberated from its Euro-American roots in order to serve Native American self-determination. Alsup believed that a liberation psychology was needed to confront traditional psychology and the oppressive conditions in society by becoming involved in creative social activism.

Acknowledgment of Social Inequalities

Mainstream counsellors emphasise the importance of personal responsibility in all aspects of life. Traditional psychology stresses the need for an individual to adjust to society's demands, but neglects to deal with inequality, powerlessness, oppression or marginality. Liberation psychology, however, emphasises that there are gross inequalities in society so that some people are highly favoured and privileged while others are disadvantaged and marginalised. The status of any individual is an outcome of many factors including gender, race, class, religion, sexual orientation, disability, age, occupation and income (Moane: 1999, 2). Responsibility is viewed by liberation psychologists as resting with both the individual and the society in which he or she lives. Oppressive regimes that inflict violence and poverty must accept ultimate responsibility for the pain and distress caused to its citizens.

Mainstream counsellors also advocate personal choice and agency. According to Moane in "Gender and Colonialism: A Psychological Analysis of Oppression and Liberation" (1999, 7), the choices available to individuals are influenced considerably by their status in society, especially in the areas of class and gender. A person growing up in poverty will spend his or her time in environments characterised by deprivation—poor housing, inadequately resourced schools, and deprived neighbourhoods. A person growing up in an affluent family will spend time in enriched environments. Gender will also shape one's environment: subjects offered in school may differ, girls may have less access to sports, and the expectations of parents with regard to each sex may be different. Social context is therefore shaped by class and gender, and also by race, ethnicity, disability, and sexual orientation. Personal choice may be greatly limited depending on one's social position.

Preoccupation with the Self

Counselling and psychotherapy have come under heavy criticism from liberation psychologists, feminists and others for their obsessive preoccupation with the self and with feelings that these practices encourage. Kitzinger and Perkins (1993) argue that too many women enter therapy for feelings such as depression and alienation, which can clearly be linked with oppression. These women are then encouraged to focus on their childhood, becoming enmeshed in endless analysis of their feelings. Kitzinger and Perkins (1993) are highly critical of mainstream counselling for advocating the client-therapist relationship as the path to liberation and growth. They argue that friendship and community are undermined by women who seek support from therapists rather than from each other.

Reconciling Opposites

Toomey (1999) developed a liberation psychology in response to the sexism that permeates traditional psychology and much of mainstream psychotherapy. Toomey (1999) claims that traditional psychology views the sexes as being unequal and, as the very term "opposite sex" suggests, opposing one another. This tradition also incorrectly interprets opposite traits within the person as being unequal, and differentiates these traits along gender lines.

According to Toomey (1999) liberation psychology rejects the assumption that opposite means hostile or unequal, and that power means control. It looks at the paradoxical relationships within the self's inner world, such as logic and emotion, as being equally legitimate forces. It teaches communication and self-expression for discovery, and not as a means of control.

Toomey's liberation psychology is a theoretical orientation that assumes our relationship to ourselves and to others is one of accord not conquest. Power is no longer seen in terms of strength and control, but in terms of energy and force. According to Toomey (1999) this framework can be applied to our whole paradoxical nature, and not just to gender.

Rejecting Psychotherapeutic Neutrality

Hollander (1997, 17) states that liberation psychologists working in Central and South America from the 1970s rejected the notion of psychotherapeutic neutrality, in the same vein that they rejected the possibility of political neutrality. Psychologists working in Chile, in Nicaragua and in Argentina, found themselves in the midst of the most appalling poverty, human suffering and widespread atrocities. Many psychologists chose to work in public hospitals and community clinics, and to treat those who had no resources to pay for psychotherapy. They began to put their professional skills at the service of those engaged in the radical transformation of society.

Patients told of appalling torture and rape being inflicted, of family members disappearing, of massacres and bombings, and of dreadful living conditions. Many psychotherapists became involved in the political struggle for the overthrow of the corrupt and barbaric juntas that oppressed these poverty-stricken people. According to Hollander (1997, 17), there is no place for professional neutrality when oppressive social regimes exploit, terrorise and murder thousands of innocent people.

Acknowledging Injustice

Martin-Baro (1994), a psychologist in El Salvador, argued that Central America, a region enmeshed in military repression, civil wars, and liberation struggles, demanded a new psychology—a liberation psychology. This new psychology would free itself from old individualistic and scientific models and instead become an ally in the people's struggle for emancipation. Martin-Baro (1994, xi) claimed that either psychology accepts or opposes inequality in society. Liberation psychology does not abstract subjects from their social and political contexts. To be beneficial both personally and socially, psychology and psychotherapy must acknowledge economic exploitation, social injustice, political oppression, terror, war, violence, and clearly make a stand against them. This is in stark contrast to mainstream counselling and psychotherapy which claims to be value-free, and which has never mobilised its members into political action or social reform.

SUMMARY

This chapter provided a review of liberation psychology. It outlined how liberation psychology challenges the counselling of oppressed people in mainstream counselling and focuses on the need for social as well as personal change. It explored the roots of liberation psychology and outlined a liberation psychology framework. It then looked at liberation psychology and counselling, and addressed such issues as the need for social change, acknowledging social inequalities, counselling's preoccupation with the self, reconciling opposites, rejecting psychotherapeutic neutrality, and acknowledging injustice.

The final chapter provides a brief summary of the overall findings. It also highlights key areas where change is urgently required if counselling is to grow, develop and transform into a truly caring, healing and empowering profession.

The Way Forward

Principal Critiques of Mainstream Counselling

There have been many complaints levelled against counsellors and counselling in the previous chapters from a plethora of researchers and alternative practitioners. These are briefly summarised below.

Counselling as a Form of Exploitation

Researchers have questioned the very nature and purpose of counselling and psychotherapy (Dineen: 1998; Masson: 1988; Smail: 1978; Charlton: 1998; Carlton: 1995; Striano: 1988; Szasz: 1961). The question is asked: does counselling actually do anything to alleviate a client's distress or to bring about effective change? Research into the affects of counselling on clients shows that counselling is no more effective than having no treatment at all (Dineen: 1998; Rowan: 1992). Therapy is by its very nature an artificial relationship and is little more than a business transaction (Masson: 1988, 229; Dineen: 1998). Counsellors have been accused of encouraging clients' dependency, and of manipulating and exploiting them by insisting on long-term counselling (Carlson: 1995; Striano: 1988). Counselling has been called a cult, a confidence trick, and counsellors have been accused of using brainwashing techniques on their clients (Charlton: 1998). Counselling has been viewed as an insidious form of social control (Szasz: 1961).

Abuse of Power

The abuse of power by the counsellor during counselling has been highlighted by many researchers (Smail: 1978; Worell and Remer:1992, 94; Kaschak: 1981; Sue and Sue: 1981, 69; Cade and O'Hanlon: 1993; Dineen: 1998). Although counselling was originally established as a reaction to antiquated and authoritarian mental health care treatments, criticisms of present-day counselling state that counsellor's do little to puncture their public image of 'expert' in the areas of human behaviour (Smail: 1978). Feminist counsellors also criticise mainstream counsellors for their adherence to sex-role stereotypes and institutionalised sexism (Worell and Remer: 1992, 92). Researchers have also reported sexist and abusive practices in counselling (Masson: 1988; Dineen: 1998).

The Need to Promote Social Change

Critiques of counselling have frequently focused on its failure to acknowledge the need for social change (Chaplin: 1992; Sue and Sue: 1981; Moane: 1999; Landfield: 1975) while obsessing over the client's responsibility for personal change (Pedersen: 1987; Puniamurthy: 2000; Kitzinger and Perkins: 1993). Social, economic and political inequalities and injustices, oppression engendered by classism and racism, and the importance of culture in shaping and creating clients' environments and worldviews are largely non-existent in the literature of mainstream counselling (Chaplin: 1992; Sue and Sue: 1981; Jones: 1978; Mohamed and Smith (cited by Laurence: 1997); Markowitz: 1994; Puniamurthy: 2000; Chapman: 1988; Moane, 1999; Alsup: 2000; Hollander: 1997; Martin-Baro:1994). Liberation psychologists, feminists and cross-cultural counsellors view this as a serious flaw of mainstream counselling, as individuals need the support of a safe, just and caring environment in order to function fully and healthily as members of any society.

Counselling Theories and Methods

The theories and methods of mainstream counselling have been critiqued by several researchers (Smail: 1978; Masson 1988; Dineen: 1998). Criticism falls on the wide range of contrasting theories that counsellor's practice that are frequently in marked opposition to each other (Smail: 1978), on the artificial nature of the counselling relationship, where counsellor's are paid by clients for providing an intimate service (Masson: 1988), and of the impossibility of teaching the skills of empathy and understanding to counsellor trainees (Smail: 1978; Calia: 1966).

Value-free Counselling

Mainstream counselling literature refers to counselling as a non-judgemental and value-free relationship. This is clearly refuted (Masson: 1988, 294; Worell and Remer: 1992, 4; Hurvitz: 1947), as it is suggested that counsellor's values influence every area of their work. Most counsellors' backgrounds tend to be white, western and middle-class, so that their values reflect their class and culture. Therefore researchers suggest that there is great difficulty in counsellors being open to clients who come from different cultures, class or gender. Counsellors usually hold stereotypical views of non-western clients, and are often not even aware of doing so (Atkinson et al: 1989; Ivey, Bradford-Ivey, and Simek-Downing, 1996; Katz, 1985; Sue and Sue: 1981; Chaplin: 1992; Lewis: 1966; Puniamurthy: 2000).

Similarity of Counsellor and Client

Research has asserted that similarity of counsellor and client, in terms of culture, class, sexual orientation and gender, is an important ingredient in the success of the counselling relationship, as it greatly affects empathy, sensitivity, and basic communication (Guntrip: 1969; Gonsiorek: 1985, 23; Riddle and Sang: 1978; Dickson: 1989; Calia: 1966; Jones: 1978; Mohamed and Smith (cited by Laurence: 1977, 135); Markowitz: 1994; Sue and Sue 1981 and 1988; Chapman: 1988; Puniamurthy: 2000). Counsellor's who deny that similarity is an issue and who try to ignore the importance of understanding cross-cultural clients often alienate their clients while blaming them for their lack of co-operation (Richardson, 1981; Trimble, 1981).

SO WHERE TO NOW?

To completely right off all counselling however as a complete hoax, a fraud or a cult seems to be a little premature. People have always needed someone to listen to their pain, to their stories, to their dreams and their disasters. The priest, the elder, the shaman and the healer have answered this call in other times and in other cultures. However, it is frequently the counsellor who is expected to play these and other roles in western society today. Whether this is partly due to counsellors' advertisement of themselves as 'expert' is open to conjecture. Counsellors must be aware, however, of client's expectations, where they are seen as spiritual directors by those who search for meaning in life, as friends by those who feel alienated and unloved, devoid of community and a sense of belonging, and as well-balanced authorities who have all the answers to life's tragedies and dilemmas. It is important for counsellors not to interpret this as the loneliness of a frustrated or introverted client, but to move beyond the individual to the changes in society that have brought about such breakdown and isolation in family life, in the workplace, in the loss of communities and religious practices.

Perhaps also it is vital for counsellors not to promise the sun, moon and stars to clients who wish for huge transformation. There is a growing need for counsellors to show themselves as human beings who are not infallible. Counsellors are ordinary people who have studied various counselling techniques, who have delved inside themselves to search for understanding and answers to their own pain, and who now wish to work with others to help them gain insight into their past, and to develop a life path which is conducive to their needs and goals. For counsellors as a profession to begin to speak of their limitations and vulnerabilities will perhaps be the most radical move forward towards transformation and growth.

The critiques of mainstream counselling which this book has identified centre on three main features of counselling, and indicate several desirable changes in the realm of counselling which may contribute to its transformation: training, an exploration of the motivation to become a counsellor, and in the area of research.

Training

The first issue is that counsellors are not sufficiently trained in certain crucial areas of human interaction, and that they have little awareness of the affects of social inequalities and injustice on clients' psychological wellbeing. The training of counsellor's should include the counselling of clients from different cultures, class, gender and sexual orientation. Problems that result from lack of similarity in the counselling relationship should be thoroughly explored. Likewise the merits of minority cultures that the counsellor may be unfamiliar with should be acknowledged, and various projects should be undertaken to gain a greater understanding of beliefs and practices in other cultures.

The importance of social, economic and political factors in shaping an individual's life should be brought to the forefront of the therapeutic relationship. Certainly personal responsibility can be explored hand in hand with social responsibility in terms of the roots of behaviour, feeling and thoughts, and one's specific choices or options. But the fact that many people have limited choice due to the social or economic constrains imposed by their environment must be acknowledged. In this way both personal responsibility and social responsibility may be investigated. The roots of personal trauma in terms of individual relationships as well as social context may be explored.

The core of this kind of relationship is client empowerment. Clients are helped to develop clarity and awareness as to the real issues that are impinging on their lives, such as hierarchical work structures, abusive family upbringing, discrimination, or alcoholism. Behaviour at an individual as well as a social level can then be discussed. Clients are then encouraged to devise manageable personal goals to help them deal with particular problems they are experiencing.

It is assumed that the training of counsellors in gender, social and cultural issues will increase individual counsellor's awareness and sensitivity to the impact on clients who may live in very different situations to the counsellor. Also it must be emphasised that counselling can never be a value-free and psychologically neutral activity. Counsellors must learn to examine their own values regarding culture, race, class, gender and other individual characteristics which may differ from their clients' worldviews. It is imperative for counsellors to learn, from research and from introspection, that these values have the potential to greatly influence the whole therapeutic relationship, and indeed to destroy the counselling relationship if they remain unacknowledged.

Motivation to Become a Counsellor

The second issue in mainstream counselling concerns people's motivation in becoming counsellors, and also their attitude to and treatment of clients. Issues which need to be dealt with thoroughly in the training and assessment of clients include the reasons why people train to become counsellors, and the potential for abuse. It must be clearly stated and discussed that abuse of power is a common phenomenon. Counsellors may wish to believe that they are immune from such tendencies, but surely a profession which works daily with the vagaries and complexity of the human heart, mind and soul must surely be used to the practices of self-delusion and the deep desire to cover ones own feelings of inadequacy with those of superiority.

The potential for abuse must be acknowledged to be in all relationships, especially those where one person (the client) is vulnerable and in need of emotional help and guidance, and the other person (the counsellor) is all too often viewed as a life expert. This certainly does not imply that there is abuse in all relationships, but it does suggest that power needs to be carefully monitored and those wielding it must be persistently coached as to ruthless self-examination of their use of power on a daily basis.

One's motivations to become a counsellor may be conscious or unconscious. It may include altruistic motivation, the need to find a career and a source of income, or the desire to have power over those who are vulnerable. The potential abusive practices in counselling, as well as counsellors' superior attitude, can seriously damage and alienate clients. These problem areas should be emphasised in the statement of ethics of each school of counselling. Individual motivation should be an important part of assessing people's suitability to train as counsellors. These issues should be frequently discussed during training, and not just briefly mentioned, as is all too often the case. Research in this regard clearly states that any abuse of power on the part of the counsellor is a particularly insidious and widespread problem (Masson: 88; Cade and O'Hanlon: 1993; Dineen: 1998; Vesel-Mander and Kent-Rush: 1974; Worell and Remer: 1992; kaschak: 1981; Puniamurthy: 2000; Sue and Sue: 1981). It is therefore imperative that all schools of counselling emphasise the potential for abuse and disrespectful behaviour toward clients, especially those from a different culture, class, or educational background than the counsellor.

Research

The third issue is the type of research that should be conducted to ascertain whether clients receive benefit from counselling, and if so which particular schools of counselling or counsellor characteristics ensure the greatest success in counselling. Evidence from research into the affects of counselling has so far produced mixed results (Dineen: 1998; Bergin: 1971; Emrick: 1977; Luborsky, Singer and Luborsky: 1975; Smith and Glass: 1977; Osipow: 1980: 200; Trux and Mitchell: 1977). Many researchers have concluded that clients' views on the whole area of counselling have not been taken into account (Saunders: 1999; Polkinghorne: 1984). Very few researchers have attempted to conduct research that asks clients what they think about the therapy they are receiving (McLeod: 1998; Rowan: 1992). Therefore research which deals less with quantitative techniques, and concentrates upon more open qualitative methods to ascertain the actual affects of counselling on clients across culture, class, gender, and sexual orientation could be very beneficial in discovering whether, or in what circumstances, counselling is viewed as a positive experience by the client.

When conducting research, it is of the utmost importance that the power exerted by social researchers is acknowledged. Firstly there is the question of which group is funding and conducting the research, and what is the aim in doing so. If there is a desired outcome, for example, that counselling is 'proven' to be effective in helping clients deal with certain crises, then there may be inbuilt bias in the research from the very beginning. Secondly, there may be bias used in the type of subjects selected to partake in the research. Thirdly there may be further bias inherent in the language used to illicit subject responses.

According to McLeod (2001), qualitative research is the way forward for counsellors and psychotherapists to begin to understand the complexities of the therapeutic process. This can be achieved by using qualitative research methods that seek to explore the meaning of a client's actual experience in counselling. Methods include eliciting people's stories through conversation, discourse or narrative, so that a client's world can be described, analysed and interpreted. In qualitative research there is a greater awareness of barriers such as gender, class, ethnicity and power that may inhibit professionals from gaining a rich understanding of their client's world. Qualitative researchers try their utmost to give clients a voice, where their true experiences can be documented. In quantitative statistical research the investigator exerts a high level of control over what subjects say, whereas with qualitative research there is a more collaborative approach, since researchers usually have some kind of dialogue with their subjects.

Also the issue of the most beneficial timeframe of counselling needs to be researched. There are many questions that need to be addressed here, for example, is there an optimum number of hours or sessions in which clients make greatest progress? Is it during the initial stages of counselling that clients gain most insights? When is there a danger that a client will become dependent on counselling and will continue to pay the counsellor although little or no benefit is occurring?

It would also be of benefit to conduct research into the code of ethics, and also into the complaints procedures that counselling schools advocate for counsellors and clients. The welfare of the client must be emphasised at all times, and all safeguards must be taken to maintain the highest degree of integrity in the therapeutic relationship.

SUMMARY

Critiques of mainstream counselling have been made by feminist counsellors, cross-cultural counsellors and liberation psychologists. General criticisms have come from researchers and psychotherapists who have become dissatisfied with the theories and practices of mainstream counselling. The principal criticisms focus on abuse of power, the need to promote social change, counselling theories and methods, value-free counselling, and the similarity of counsellor and client.

The way forward for counselling appears to centre on the training of counsellors as to the affects of social inequalities and injustices on client's psychological well-being, in terms of culture, class, gender and sexual orientation. A new social awareness by counsellors is required that not only allows but actively encourages clients to explore and name the reality of their day-to-day lives. Counsellors' awareness of the damage to clients by abusive practices, and the alienation of clients by counsellors' superior attitude must also be emphasised in training, and by an examination of trainees' motivation to practice as counsellors.

Conducting qualitative research as to the effectiveness of counselling, and documenting client's actual experiences of the counselling process, is another important step in informing us of how best counselling can serve its clients. Acknowledging that research is often plagued with bias, power-issues and control is vital for conducting a new kind of research that is more collaborative and client-centred. It is the client's voice that needs to be heard, the client's experience of counselling that needs to be described and shared, in order that counselling can grow and prosper into a just therapeutic intervention for all.

Notes

1. Today there are hundreds of schools of counselling which offer their services to individuals, couples and families. In the 1980s there were well over 250 different schools of counselling reported by Corsini (1981) and Hendrik (1980). These included the most common forms of counselling: person-centred counselling, gestalt therapy, and reality therapy. The term mainstream counselling refers collectively to these and other widely practiced forms of counselling.

2. Behaviourism is an approach to psychology that emphasises observable measurable behaviour. It was pioneered by Pavlov, a physiologist, at the beginning of the twentieth century. Pavlov developed classical conditioning as a central hypothesis of behaviourism, which postulates that learning can be explained through a complex series of stimulus-response connections.

3. Psychoanalysis was developed by Freud in the late 1890s. At the root of psychoanalysis is the assumption of the existence of unconscious mental processes that follow laws, which do not apply, to conscious thinking. Free association, dream interpretation and analysis of resistance and transference are used by an analyst to explore the patient's repressed unconscious impulses, anxieties and internal conflicts. Psychoanalysis is part of the psychodynamic school, which focuses on the study, and treatment of the subconscious.

4. Psychotherapy and counselling are terms, which are frequently used interchangeably. Psychotherapy refers to a deep exploration into the roots of the client's past experiences, seeking to bring about lasting changes by healing old traumas and hurts.

5. Cognitive psychology examines internal mental processes such as problem solving, memory, and language. Cognitive psychologists are interested in how people understand, diagnose, and solve problems, concerning themselves with the mental processes which mediate between stimulus and response. Cognitive theory contends that solutions to problems take the

form of algorithms or rules that are not necessarily understood but promise a solution.

6. ECT is the administering of electroconvulsive therapy, or shock treatment.

7. Etiology refers to the cause of a problem.

References

Adler, A. (1956), *The Individual Psychology of Alfred Adler*, ed. H and R Ansbacher, Basic Books, New York

Agoro, A (2003), 'Anti-racist Counselling Practice', in C. Largo and B. Smith (eds), Anti-discriminatory Counselling Practice, Sage, London

Alsup, R.E (2000), *Liberation Psychology: A Visionary Mandate for Humanistic, Existential and Transpersonal Psychologies*, Web site: **www.sonoma.edu/psychology/os2db/alsup1.html**

Atkinson, D. R., Furlong, M. J., Poston, W. C., & Mercado, P. (1989), '*Ethnic group preferences for counsellor characteristics*', Journal of Counselling Psychology, *36*, 68-72

Atkinson, D.R, Thompson, C.E, and Grant, S.K (1993), '*A Three-Dimentional Model for Counselling Racial/Ethnic Minorities*', Counselling Psychologist, 21(2), 257-277

Ballou, M. B and Gabalac, N. W (1985), *A Feminist Position on Mental Health*, Charles C. Thomas, Springfield, Illinois

Baker-Miller, J (1976), *Toward a New Psychology of Women*, Penguin, London

Bergin, A.E (1971), '*The Evaluation of Therapeutic Outcomes*', in A.E Bergin and S.L Garfield (eds.) Handbook of Psychotherapy and Behaviour Changes, Wiley, New York

Berry, J.W. (1969), '*On Cross-cultural Comparability*', International Journal of Psychology, Vol. 4, 119-128, Canada

Brunswick, R,M (1928), '*The Analysis of a Jealousy Illusion*', International Journal of Psychoanalysis, Vol 14, p 458

Budman, S.H, and Gurman, A.S, (1988), *Theory and Practice of Brief Therapy,* Hutchinson, London

Burn, D. (1992), *'Ethical Implications in Cross-Cultural Counselling and Training'.* Journal of Counselling and Development, Vol. 70, 578-583

Cade, B, and O'Hanlon, W (1993), *A Brief Guide of Brief Therapy,* W.W. Norton, New York

Calia, V.F (1966), *'The Culturally Deprived Client: A Reformulation of the Counsellor's role',* Journal of Counselling Psychology, 13, 100-105

Carlson, R (1995), *Shortcut Through Therapy,* Plume, New York

Chaplin, J, (1992), *Feminist Counselling in Action,* Sage Publications, London

Charlton, B (1998), *The Counselling Cult,* from LM issue 112

Chodorow, N (1978), *The Reproduction of Mothering,* University of California Press, Berkeley, California

Corsini, R.J (1981), *Handbook of Innovative Psychotherapies,* John Wiley and Sons, New York

Dineen, T (1998), *Manufacturing Victims: What the Psychology Industry is Doing to People,* Constable, London

Dinnerstein, D (1978), *The Rocking of the Cradle,* Souvenir Press, London

De Beauvoir, S (1949), *The Second Sex,* Gallimard, Paris, France

Deloria, V. (1983), *American Indians, American Justice,* University of Texas Press, Austin, Texas

Daly, M (1986), *Beyond God the Father,* Women's Press, London

Das, A.K 1995, *'Rethinking Multicultural Counselling: Implications for Counsellor Education',* in Journal of Counselling and Development, 74 (1), 45-52

Dickson, A (1989), *The Mirror Within: A New Look at Sexuality,* Quartet Books, London

Dominelli, L. (1988), *Anti-Racist Social Work,* Macmillan, London

Dryden, W (1987), *Key Cases in Psychotherapy,* New York University Press, Washington Square, New York

Dryden, W (Ed), (1996), *Handbook of Individual Therapy in Britain.* London, Sage

Egan G (1998), *The Skilled Helper,* Brooks/Cole Publishing Company, Pacific Grove, California

Emrick CD (1975), '*A Review of Psychologically Oriented Treatment in Alcoholism',* Journal of Studies of Alcohol, 36, 88-108

Feltham, C (1997), *Time-Limited Counselling,* Sage Publications, London

Feltham, C, and Dryden, W (1994), *Developing Counsellor Training,* Sage Publications, London

Fernando, S (1988), *Race and Culture in Psychiatry,* Routledge, London

Firestone, S (1949), *The Dialectic of Sex,* Women's Press, London

Friedan, B (1977), *The Feminine Mystique,* Dell, New York

Gelso, C. J., and Hayes, J. A. (1998), *The Psychotherapy Relationship: Theory Research and Practice,* John Wiley and Sons, New York

Greenberg, L. G. (1981), 'Advances in Clinical Intervention Research: A decade review', *Canadian Psychology, 22*(1), 25-34

Glasser, W (1984), *Control Theory: A New Explanation of How we Control our Lives,* Perennial Library, New York

Glasser, W (1965), *Reality Therapy: A New Approach to Psychiatry,* Harper and Row, New York

Goffman, E (1961), *Asylums: Essays on the Social Situation of Mental Patients and their Inmates,* Doubleday and Co. Garden City, New York

Gonsiorek, J.C (ed) (1985), *Homosexuality and Psychotherapy,* The Haworth Press, New York

Graves, R (1955), *The Greek Myths,* Vols 1 and 2, Pelican, Harmondstown

Greenspan, M (1983), *A New Approach to Women and Therapy,* McGraw-Hill, New York

Greer, G (1971), *The Female Eunuck,* Paladin, London

Guntrip, H (1969), *Schizoid Phenomena, Object Relations and the Self,* International Universities Press, New York

Hendrik, R (1981), *The Psychotherapy Handbook,* Meridian Books, New York

Hollander, N C (1997), *Love in a Time of Hate*: Liberation Psychology in Latin America, Rutgers University Press, New Jersey

Hollingshead, A.B, and Redlich, F.C (1958), *Social Class and Mental Illness,* Wiley, New York

Hopson, B (1981), *Counselling and Helping in Psychology and Medicine,* ed. David Griffiths, British Psychological Society, and The Macmillan Press Ltd, Basingstoke

Hopton, J. and Williams, S. (1994), 'Counselling and Social Justice', Asylum: Magazine for Democratic Psychiatry, 8 (2), pp. 19-20

Horney, K (1924), *'On the Genesis of the Castration Complex in Women',* International Journal of Psychoanalysis, 5, Reprinted in Horney, Feminine Psychology, Routledge & Kegan Paul, London, 1967

Howard, A (1996), *Challenges to Counselling and Psychotherapy,* Macmillan, London

Hurvitz, N (1974), *'Psychotherapy as a Means of Control',* in Journal and Consulting and Clinical Psychology, 40, 237

Ivey, A, Bradford-Ivey, M, and Simek-Morgan, L (1996), *Counselling and Psychotherapy: A Multicultural Perspective,* Allyn and Bacon, Boston

Kaschak, E (1981), *'Feminist Psychotherapy: The First Decade',* from S. Cox (Ed.), Female Psychology: The Emerging Self, St. Martin's Press, New York

Katz, J (1985), *The Philosophy of Linguistics,* Oxford, New York

Kitzinger C., and Perkins, R. (1993), *Changing Our Minds: A Radical Lesbian Critique of Psychology and its Dangers*, Onlywomen Press, London

Klein, M (1932), *The Psychoanalysis of Children*, Hogarth, London

Landfield, A (1975), *'The Complaint: A Confrontation of Personal Urgency and Professional Construction'*. In D. Bannister (ed.), Issues and Approaches in the Psychological Therapies, Wiley, London and New York

Laurence, M (ed) (1997*), Psychotherapy with Women: Feminist Perspectives*, Macmillan, Basingstoke

Lester, E.P (1990), *'Gender and Identify Issues in the Analytic Process'*, International Journal of Psychoanalysis, 71:435-44

Lerman, H (1976), *'What Happens in Feminist Therapy?'* from S. Cox (Ed), Female Psychology: The Emerging Self, Chicago: Science Research Associates

Lewis, O (1966), *'The Culture of Poverty'*, Scientific American, Vol. 215, Number 4, 19-25

Lewis, Ronald G. and Keung Ho (1975), *'Managing Social Work with Native Americans'*, Social Work, Sept; 20(5), 379-382

Luepnitz, D (1988), *The Family Interpreted*, Basic Books, New York

Luborsky, L, Singer, B and Luborsky, (1975), *'Comparative Studies of Psychotherapies'*, Archives of General Psychiatry, 32, 995-1008

MacLeod, L (1990), *Counselling for Change: Evolutionary Trends in Counselling Services for Women who are Abused and for their Children in Canada*, for the National Clearinghouse on Family Violence Prevention Division, Health and Welfare Canada, Tuinney's Pasture, Ottawa, Ontario K1A 1B5

Mann, B, (1987), *'Validation or Liberation? A Critical Look at Therapy and the Women's Movement'*, Trivia, 10, 41-56

Marcos, L, Uruyo, L, Kesselman, M, and Alpert, M (1973), *'The Language Barrier in Evaluating Spanish-American Patients'*, Arch. General Psychiatry, Vol. 29, 655-659

Markowitz, L.M (1994), '*The Cross-Currents of Multiculturalism*', in The Family Therapy Networker, 18(4), 187-192

Martin-Baro, I (1994), *Writings for a Liberation Psychology*, Harvard University Press, Cambridge, Massachusetts

Masson, J, (1988), *Against Therapy*, Fontana, London

Mehrabian, A (1972), *Nonverbal Communication*, Aldine-Atherson, Chicago, Illinois

McFadden, J and Wilson T (1977), *Non-white Academic Training within Counsellor Education*, Rehabilitation Counselling and Student Personnel Programs, Unpublished Research

Mcleod, J. (1998), *An Introduction to Counselling* (2nd ed.), Open University Press, Buckingham

McLeod, J. (2001), *Qualitative Research in Counselling and Psychotherapy*, Sage Publications, London

Millet, K, (1969), *Sexual Politics*, Rupert Hart-Davis, London

Mitchell, J (1975), *Psychoanalysis and Feminism*, Penguin, Harmondsworth

Moane, G (1999), *The Concept of a Liberation Psychology*, Department of Psychology, University College Dublin, Ireland

Moane, G., (1999), *Gender and Colonialism: A Psychological Analysis of Oppression and Liberation*, St. Martin's Press, New York

Murgatroyd, S (1985), *Counselling and Helping*, British Psychological Society and Methuen, London

Newsome, A (1980), '*Doctors and Counsellors in Collaboration or Conflict*', in Counselling News, British Association for Counselling and Psychotherapy, UK, No. 34, Sept. 1980

Norcross, J. C., & Prochaska, J. O. (1983), 'Contemporary Psychotherapists: A National Survey of Characteristics, Practices, Orientations and Attitudes', *Psychotherapy: Theory, Research and Practice*, 20(2), 161-173

O'Farrell, Ursula (1988), *First Steps in Counselling*, Veritas, Dublin

O'Leary, E (1992), *Gestalt Therapy: Theory, Practice and Research*, Chapman and Hall, London

Orbach, S (1993), *Hunger Strike*, Penguin, London

Palmer, S and Varma, V (eds.) (1997), *The Future of Counselling and Psycho-therapy*, Sage Publications, London

Parry, S. M (1984), '*Feminist Therapy*', from Encyclopedia of Psychology Vol 2, John Wiley and Sons, New York

Peavy, R.V. (1977), *Adults helping adults: An Existential Approach to Cooperative Counselling*, Victoria, British Columbia, Canada

Peavy, R.V. (1979), '*Therapy and creativity: A dialogue*'. The Journal of Creative Behaviour Vol 13, 60-71

Peavy, R.V (1988), *Credo for Counsellors: Sociodynamic Counselling*, Mitt Gorlag, Malmo, Sweden

Peavy, R.V. (1988), *Sociodynamic Counselling,* Department of Psychological Foundations, University of Victoria, British Columbia, Canada

Pedersen, P. (1987), *Handbook of Cross Cultural Counselling and Therapy*, Prae-ger, USA

Pedersen, P. (1994), *A Handbook for Developing Multicultural Awareness* (2nd ed.), American Counselling Association, Alexandria, Virginia

Pedersen P. (1996) (ed.) *Counselling Across Cultures*, Sage Publications Inc, USA

Perls, F. (1969), *Gestalt Therapy Verbatim*, Bantom Books, New York

Perls, F. (1969), *In and Out of the Garbage Pail*, Real People Press, Lafayette, California

Persaud, R. (1996), 'The Wisest Counsel?', Counselling, 7 (3), pp. 199-201

Philips D, and Rathwell, T. (1986), *Health, Race and Ethnicity*, Routledge Kegan & Paul, London

Polkinghorne, D. E. (1984*), 'Further extensions of methodological diversity for counselling psychology',* Journal of Counselling Psychology, Vol. 31, 416-429

Puniamurthy, K. (2000), *'Using Cross-Cultural Counselling to Serve Diverse Student Populations: A Malaysian Perspective',* 7th Asia Pacific Student Association (APSSA), International Conference, Manila, Philippines

Rawlings, E. I., & Carter, D. K (1977*), Psychotherapy for Women: Treatment towards Equality,* Thomas, Springfield, Illinois

Reich, J. (1970), *The Mass Psychology of Fascism,* Pelican, London

Richardson, E.H. (1981),*'Cultural and Historical Perspectives in Counselling American Indians',* in D.W. Sue (Ed.), Counselling the Culturally Different, 216-255, John Wiley and Sons, New York

Riddle, D.I and Sang, B (1978), '*Psychotherapy with Lesbians',* in Journal of Social Issues, 34, 84-100

Rogers, C (1961), *On Becoming a Person,* Houghton Mifflin, Boston

Rosenthal, D (1955), '*Changes in Some Moral Values Following Psychotherapy',* in Journal of Consulting Psychology, 19, 431-36

Rowan, J. (1992), 'In a response to, Mair, K: The myth of therapist expertise', in W. Dryden & C. Feltham (Eds.), *Psychotherapy and its discontents* (pp. 160-166), Open University Press, Buckingham, England

Ruth, S (1988), *'Understanding Oppression and Liberation',* Studies, Vol. 77, No. 308, Winter, pp. 434-444

Saunders L (1999*), 'It has been Amply Demonstrated that Psychotherapy is Effective',* in C. Feltham (Ed.), *Controversies in Psychotherapy and Counselling* (pp. 294-302), London: Sage

Serpell R. (1978), *Culture's Influence on Behaviour,* Richard Clay Ltd, England

Sherrard, C (1991), Unpublished paper presented to members of the British Psychology Society, Lincoln, England

Smail, D. (1978), *Psychotherapy: A Personal Approach*, J.M. Dent & Sons, London

Smail, D. (1987), *Taking Care: The Limits of Therapy,* Verso, London

Smith, M.C, and Glass, G.U, (1977*), 'Meta-Analysis of Psychological Outcome Studies',* American Psychologist, 32, 752-776

Starhawk (1990), *Dreaming the Dark: Magic, Sex and Politics*, Mandala—Unwin Hyman Ltd., London

Striano, J (1988), *Can Psychotherapists Hurt You?,* Professional Press, Santa Barbara, California

Sturdivant, S (1980), *Therapy with Women: A Feminist Philosophy of Treatment*, Springer, New York

Sue, DW and Sue, D (1981), *Counselling the Culturally Different*, John Wiley & Sons, New York

Sussman, M.B., (1992), A Curious Calling: Unconscious Motivations for Practicing Psychotherapy, Jason Aronson, Northvale, New Jersey

Thomas A, and Sillen, S (1972*), Racism and Psychiatry*, Brunner/Mazel, New York

Toomey, M (1999), *The Evolution of Liberation Psychology*, Web site: **www.mtoomey.com**

Trimble, J.E. (1981), *'Value differentials and their importance in counselling American Indians',* In P.P. Pederson et al. (Eds.) Counselling Across Cultures, 2nd edition. Honolulu: University of Hawaii Press

Trux, C.B, and Mitchell, K. M (1971), *'Research on Certain Therapist Interpersonal Skills in Relations to Process and Outcome',* in A.E Bergin and S.L Garfield (eds.), Handbook of Psychotherapy and Behaviour Changes, Wiley, New York

Vesel-Mander, A, and Kent-Rush, A, (1974), *Feminism as Therapy*, Random House, Inc., New York

Walsh, D, and Liddy, R (1989), *Surviving Sexual Abuse,* Attic Press, Dublin

Wiemann, J, and Harrison, R (1983), *Nonverbal Interaction*, Sage Publications, Beverley Hills, California, USA

Wolfgang, A (1985), *Nonverbal Behaviour: Perspectives, Applications, Intercultural Insights,* C.T Hogrefe, Toronto, Canada

Wolfe, N (1991), *The Beauty Myth*, Vintage, London

Worell, J, and Remer, P (1992), *Feminist Perspectives in Therapy: An Empowerment Model for Women*, John Wiley & Sons, New York

_____Association of Humanistic Psychology, *From Maslow to the 21ˢᵗ Century, 2001*, **http://ahpweb.org/aboutahp/whatis.html**

_____Centre for Critical Psychology, University of Western Sydney, Nepean website, 1998, **http://www.uws.edu.au**

_____Irish Association for Counselling Directory, 1991, *Guide to Counselling and Therapy*, Wolfhound, Dublin

List of Counselling Organisations

Ireland

The Irish Association for Counselling and Psychotherapy

8 Cumberland Street,
Dun Laoghaire,
Co. Dublin,
Ireland
Tel: (01) 230-0061
Fax: (01) 230-0064
Email: iact@irish-counselling.ie

United Kingdom

The British Association for Counselling and Psychotherapy

BACP House,
35-37 Albert Street,
Rugby,
Warwickshire CV21 2SG,
United Kingdom
Tel: (0870) 443-5252
Fax: (0870) 443-5161
Email: bacp@bacp.co.uk

United States

American Counselling Association

5999 Stevenson Ave.,
Alexandria,
VA 22304,
USA
Tel: (703) 823-6862
Fax: (703) 823-0252
Email: ryep@counseling.org

Other books by Lucy Costigan published by iUniverse:

Winter Solstice: A Novel (2003)

Notes

Notes

Notes

Notes

0-595-30696-9

Lightning Source UK Ltd.
Milton Keynes UK
30 April 2010

153611UK00001B/54/A